teach
yourself

chi kung

teach® yourself

chi kung
robert parry

For UK order enquiries: please contact Bookpoint Ltd., 130 Milton Park, Abingdon, Oxon OX14 4SB. Telephone: +44 (0) 1235 827720. Fax: +44 (0) 1235 400454. Lines are open 09.00–18.00, Monday to Saturday, with a 24-hour message answering service. You can also order through our website www.madaboutbooks.com

For USA order enquiries: please contact McGraw-Hill Customer Services, PO Box 545, Blacklick, OH 43004-0545, USA. Telephone: 1-800-722-4726. Fax: 1-614-755-5645.

For Canada order enquiries: please contact McGraw-Hill Ryerson Ltd., 300 Water St, Whitby, Ontario L1N 9B6, Canada. Telephone: 905 430 5000. Fax: 905 430 5020.

Long renowned as the authoritative source for self-guided learning – with more than 30 million copies sold worldwide – the *Teach Yourself* series includes over 300 titles in the fields of languages, crafts, hobbies, business, computing and education.

British Library Cataloguing in Publication Data: a catalogue record for this title is available from The British Library.

Library of Congress Catalog Card Number: on file

First published in UK 2001 by Hodder Headline Ltd., 338 Euston Road, London, NW1 3BH.

First published in US 2000 by Contemporary Books, a Division of the McGraw-Hill Companies, 1 Prudential Plaza, 130 East Randolph Street, Chicago, IL 60601 USA.

The 'Teach Yourself' name is a registered trade mark of Hodder & Stoughton Ltd.

Copyright © 2001, 2003 Robert Parry

Typeset by Transet Limited, Coventry, England.
Printed in Great Britain for Hodder & Stoughton Educational, a division of Hodder Headline Ltd., 338 Euston Road, London NW1 3BH by Cox & Wyman Ltd., Reading, Berkshire.

Impression number   10 9 8 7 6 5 4 3 2 1
Year   2009 2008 2007 2006 2005 2004 2003

contents

My thanks once again, dear Ruby, for all your help.

introduction

Where there is breath there is life. This rather obvious statement is, however, an immensely important one for those who practise the art of chi kung. And within this statement, too, there is also great power.

The Buddhist monks of the Shao-lin monastery in Honan province, northern China, are renowned for their prowess and athleticism, particularly in the field of martial arts. And although chi kung – the subject of this book – is not a martial art, it is still an important element of their training because it bestows inner strength and, after many years of dedication and training helps them to achieve some truly astonishing feats. During their sell-out tours of Europe and the USA, for example, the monks routinely break rocks in two with their bare hands; or iron bars are snapped like pretzels over knees or even heads!

You will be relieved to learn that, as a reader of this book, you will not be urged to develop such skills – because there is something much more important to be found within the practice of chi kung. Indeed, the monks of Shao-lin, raising much-needed funds for their monastery by demonstrating their abilities in this way, would be the first to remind us that one of the main purposes of chi king is actually to develop mental clarity and calm. From this, the internal energies of the body become balanced and the state of health strengthens. Health is all-important! And with this great gift at our disposal anything is possible and all that human nature in its wonderful diversity aspires to can be realized – no matter how spectacular, no matter how humble.

It would be a mistake, therefore, to view chi kung as some kind of exclusive pursuit, something special for special people. On the contrary, in China and elsewhere in the East, millions of men and women, from all walks of life, of all ages and all levels of fitness, practice chi kung in their spare time. They do so in a spirit of moderation and their aims are usually to learn to relax, to maintain their health or to combat stress. In hospitals, chi kung is even used as a therapy – allowing patients to assume a far more active role in their own healing process. What's more it is remarkably easy to learn the basic techniques of chi kung, as these are based on something we all do every moment of every day of our lives – breathing.

The great English soccer player, Sir Stanley Matthews – the first footballer ever to receive a knighthood and regarded by everyone who saw him on the field as one of the greatest sporting athletes of all time – had a secret weapon, a way of training that was not only unusual but probably unique among his contemporaries. Because of this he was able to compete at the highest level at the age of 50 – at a time of life when most footballers would have long-since hung up their boots and retired. Sir Stanley lived to the age of 85, active and alert, even writing his autobiography right up to the last. Thousands of people attended his funeral in Stoke in February 2000 and a statue of him has, for many years, held pride of place in the town centre there.

What was this mysterious secret? Well, in fact, it was not so mysterious after all and was something he would, as a man of modesty and kindness, have gladly shared with anyone willing to listen. Every morning during his playing years at Blackpool, for example, he was to be seen out early on the beach, training – jogging, sprinting, stretching in the usual way one would expect of any dedicated sportsman. But he was also doing something else. He would take great trouble always to go through a special sequence of breathing exercises which, he insisted, contributed to his stamina and concentration. Sir Stanley – and although he may or may not have been familiar with the term – was doing chi kung: his own way of cultivating internal energy and health through a combination of breathing and exercise. He was an expert at it – and it worked.

Chi kung – a definition

So what exactly is chi kung? And what does it involve? When translated into English, chi kung (also often written as *qi gong*, by the way) means something like 'energy breathing' or 'energy cultivation through breath'. We have much to learn about chi later on in this book, the body's vital energy or life force, but for now it is enough to know that chi kung is a wonderful way of staying healthy and beating stress. In this, it uses a combination of the following:

- calm, regular breathing
- slow, gentle movement
- mental focus
- inner stillness.

Each of these is an attractive proposition in its own right, of course. Mental focus, inner stillness – who would not want to make room for these at some time in their daily routine! But chi kung offers more. And when combined in the exercises outlined in the following pages, all these qualities add up to something far greater than the sum of their parts.

Beginnings

Chi kung has its origins in antiquity, probably long before the days of recorded history. It is rooted in the disciplines and practices of oriental medicine and philosophy and has stood the test of time. But chi kung is also a wholly modern activity and at moments seems almost tailor made for the typical Western lifestyle as more and more people seek a means of dealing with the stresses and strains of modern living and also perhaps for something more real and meaningful in their lives. In a world of consumerism and computer-driven virtual reality, where we are manipulated and bombarded with superficiality and greed at every turn, it is refreshing to discover something as genuine and enduring as chi kung. Ultimately, chi kung can help put us back in touch with what is real and important in our lives. And what could be more important than that!

Active and passive chi kung

There is one major distinction to note when looking at the many different styles of chi kung available today. Some chi kung encourages movement of the body in order to circulate the chi, while other types, paradoxically, make use of stillness to achieve the same ends. In this book we will look at both types, which I have labelled active and passive chi kung respectively.

The early chapters of this book, therefore, (Chapters 03 through to 07) focus on active chi kung exercises, where the arms and, in some cases the feet, move gently in time to the breathing to encourage the circulation of *chi* (vital energy) around the body. We will be looking at five separate exercises that have been taken from different systems and styles, handed down by different schools or chi kung masters. I have chosen this approach for two reasons. First, the variety on display here will provide you with a good, all-round taster for many of the different styles out there. The second is that the five exercises themselves all dovetail neatly and can be used to make up a very useful sequence for daily practice. These exercises are all ones that I have learnt and practised myself over the years and which I really enjoy doing together in this way. They work for me, and so I hope they will work for you too.

You will find one whole chapter devoted to each of these exercises. I suggest you take each one separately, and learn it thoroughly before moving on to the next. This is because the apparent simplicity of these exercises belies their real, often hidden complexity. And it is precisely this hidden complexity that is the key to making them work. To put it another way, all these movements are very easy to do badly but difficult to do well. I hope you will want to do them well, of course, because that is where the magic of chi kung lies. So be patient; take them one at a time; and later, you can combine them and build them into your daily routine.

Structure

To help with this process, the chapters themselves are clearly structured. Within each one you will find a clear learning programme set out as follows:

1 A brief introduction to the exercise itself, how it works and what you can expect to achieve from it.
2 Preparation, how to set yourself up – stance, position of feet and so on.
3 Detailed instructions for each stage of the exercise, along with tips on how to overcome common errors and obstacles. This includes the all-important instructions on co-ordinating your movements to your breathing.
4 What you can expect to feel, to help you through any unexpected sensations and to make sure you are getting the most from the exercise.

5 Mental focus. This provides a number of associations that can be made with the movements themselves and enhances the experience of chi flow in the body.
6 Notes on advanced practice. Here you will find further important refinements to the exercises once the basics have been mastered.

Beyond the physical

The notes you will find under sections 4 and 5 are pertinent because chi kung is not just about physical exercise. It is also about concentration and of transforming negative feelings and unwanted emotional baggage into something more positive and useful. Also, from my experience as both a student and a teacher of exercises of this kind, I have found that it is of limited use urging people to follow any set of repetitive movements slavishly unless they actually mean something. Because chi king is a body–mind discipline, we have an excellent opportunity here to focus on positive changes in our thoughts and emotions as we work and in this way can derive enormous benefits over time.

But what about passive chi kung exercises? Chapter 08 has us turning our attention to this topic – chi kung in which there is no physical movement at all but instead energy circulation through the deep energy pathways of the body. This is achieved through a combination of controlled breathing and mental focus. Just one example of passive chi kung is given in this book, but it is a very valuable one, and contains within it many features of this kind of work that will enable you to decide on whether it is suitable for you or not.

Getting results

So what exactly can we expect from chi kung at a personal level? Well, after just a few weeks of regular practice people tend to notice a very real improvement in their overall well-being – in their sense of balance, both physical balance and mentally as well. They also tend to feel calmer and more in control of situations, less prone to extremes of emotion. As the body begins to relax, moreover, various physical processes start to improve, to become more efficient. Digestion, respiration, circulation – all these begin to function more smoothly and so, in a sense, help the body to nourish itself from the inside outwards. This is why chi kung is often referred to as an 'internal' exercise. The actual physical activity involved is usually very slight, with just small circular movements of the arms, for instance, or a gentle rocking to and fro on the feet. But inside there are lots of positive changes taking place which, over time, have a powerful cumulative effect in terms of health.

Chi kung can, of course, also be used perfectly well in conjunction with other forms of exercise. It can be viewed as an excellent means of warming up or *warming down*, for instance, after more vigorous kinds of exercise – and blends particularly well with those other disciplines which nourish the body internally such as yoga or tai chi. It is also excellent for aiding relaxation at any time of the day and in helping the body to unwind from a busy schedule. Some people even manage to fit it into a tea break at work! At the same time, however, it can also focus and improve the mental faculties, so that enthusiasts of chi kung often report increased performance and creativity in many areas of their daily lives, both at work and at play.

How long does it take to reap all these wonderful rewards? Well, for each of us it depends on one very simple equation – the amount of time we are prepared to practise. Chi kung is an activity that rewards us well for commitment. We get back from it everything that we put in; and of course the more we do put in, the greater those rewards will be.

Is it right for you?

If all this sounds perfectly wonderful, but you are still doubting whether you have the abilities to learn chi kung, don't worry! With chi kung, you simply work within your natural capabilities. There are no competitions, no prizes, no contests to win. You don't need any special clothing or apparatus to get started, and you don't need lots of space for practice, either – just about as much as it takes to spread your arms out wide. Neither does it matter if you are not entirely fit and well. Even if you cannot stand for long periods, it's OK, because all the exercises can easily be adapted to a seated posture, and so – with a few sensible modifications – can even be undertaken by the elderly or disabled. In other words, whether you are young or old, strong or not so strong, regular chi kung practice can help you to develop and improve on your present state. If you are weak, you will become less so; and if you are already blessed with strength, you will become even stronger!

At its higher levels, of course, chi kung is a vocation and a discipline that is passed on from teacher to pupil and, just like the sublime skills developed by the great Shao-lin monks, requires much dedication and learning. Even here in the West, people often go on to attend classes for many years or even embark on one-to-one tuition from a great master as part of their quest for excellence. You may or may not want to go that far with your chi kung experience, but whatever your aspirations, you can certainly start right now. This book will help you to take that first step.

01

the art of breathing

In this chapter you will learn:
- about the history and background of chi kung
- about the five elements of oriental culture
- about the nature of chi and how it moves.

Chi kung, the art of breathing, has been around a long time. After all, people have been breathing for a long time! The special method of cultivating the breath to promote the circulation of vital energy, however, combined with exercise, is undoubtedly a feature of our more recent evolution – although with chi kung we still need to speak in terms of millennia rather than centuries.

A little piece of history

Perhaps the earliest reference we have to therapeutic exercises and special 'dances' for warding off illness date from the period of the legendary Yellow Emperor, Huang Ti, who reigned perhaps as early as 2700 BCE. Huang Ti is said to have practised these dances and has come to be regarded as a kind of exemplary figure, representing the concept of 'the sage' – that is, someone able to combine great wisdom with integrity. The great classic of oriental medicine, the *Nei Jing*, which was actually written many centuries after Huang Ti lived, was dedicated to him, as if it were in some sense his knowledge that was being represented. His legendary powers, meanwhile, are said to have extended to having reigned for 100 years and to have had over 100 wives. So, a remarkable man in every respect!

By the sixth century BCE scholars had already begun to classify and discuss various methods of exercise and breathing techniques for maintaining health. Some of these movements are depicted in jade carvings dating from this time. And during what is known by historians as the Warring States Period, 480–222 BCE, a particularly fruitful and creative period of Chinese culture, we find the emergence of what are called *tao yin* (*daoyin*) disciplines, again special exercises for health that may, in part at least, have been derived from the much earlier era of the Yellow Emperor.

Tao yin means 'guiding and inducing'. And it is, of course, the movement of energy which is referred to – guiding and inducing the flow of chi around the energy pathways of the body. The point to note here is that these were exercises for both body *and* mind – and also made extensive use of the breath in order to circulate the vital energy. At the same time, special breathing techniques, combined with meditation, were also being introduced by the Taoist philosophers. These techniques, they claimed, were effective not only in the treatment of certain illnesses but also in the prevention of disease.

The philosophy of health

It is important to understand that in those times a philosopher was also someone who meditated and probably also practised medicine. All these subjects were linked. For example, the philosopher Wei Po-yang in his writings makes a very telling statement to the effect of: 'You build a wall around the city so the people will be safe.' On the face of it, this is a rather mundane kind of statement for the times, when towns and cities invariably availed themselves of walled defences, but in the context of philosophy and health it is of enormous interest. He uses a metaphor to describe the body's own defences, based on strong vital energy, the 'chi'. He is also alluding to the inextricable association between body and mind that is central to all areas of health culture in the East and clearly suggests that exercise for strengthening the body against disease is paramount in the successful practice of meditation.

It was realized at this time that all the body's internal organs and systems were interrelated and that a disturbance in any one may be the result of a malfunction in another. We will have more to say about oriental medical theory later in this book, and Taoist philosophy too, fascinating subjects in their own right and which must always be considered in the practice of chi kung. These common threads of knowledge, running through so many seemingly diverse areas of Chinese culture, make up what we would today term an 'holistic' approach, in which the mind and body, and the environment too, are all seen as interrelated.

From here on in, we start to find clear individual styles of chi kung emerging – definite landmarks along the way, such as the silk painting discovered in an ancient tomb in Hunan Province in the 1970s which shows a series of 18 forms of health exercises attributed to the alchemist Ko Hung (active around 325 CE). And just a little earlier, towards the end of the Han Dynasty, we have the famous practitioner of oriental medicine, Hua Tuo, advocating special regimes of exercise, called *wu chin hsi*, specifically in order to boost resistance to disease. This is a system which mimics the movements of animals such as the bear, the monkey or the tiger and which is still in use today. One of Hua Tuo's sayings is: 'Running water never gets stale' – a clear reference to the beneficial effects of movement and exercise on the human body.

Hau Tuo taught his movements openly and they were widely disseminated, as were, much later, another set of well-known pieces from the Song Dynasty (around the twelfth century) called the Eight Brocades, which are thought to have been developed by an army officer to maintain the internal strength of his troops. At the same time, however, other systems were being developed in secrecy among certain families or clans, usually connected to the Imperial Court which was always a centre for excellence in all the arts and sciences. Many of these exercises, moreover, developed in tandem with the martial arts. Among Buddhist communities of this era, too, we find numerous fighting arts and disciplines of self cultivation – including, for instance, the *Tai Chi Chu'an* forms which, again, are still widely practised today both for their healing and their martial qualities.

So there is your history lesson! From this illustrious past, most of the styles of chi kung that we recognize today have developed and grown, their practitioners building always upon the experiences of their predecessors. The list of examples is endless. But suffice to say that the use of exercise for maintaining health and for circulating vital energy around the body is probably one of the earliest activities recorded in the history of human civilization and has, moreover, been in continuous use for at least 4500 years. Not a bad track record, to be sure.

Learning chi kung

He who stands on tip-toe does not stand firm.
He who takes the longest strides does not walk the fastest.

Tao Te Ching

In China and Japan it is a lot easier to learn chi kung than in the West. There is always somebody you know, somebody just around the corner and you simply join in and copy what they do. You can start at an early age, as well, if you wish, because it is also taught in schools. You can find it in colleges, in workers' clubs, in city parks and even in hospitals and clinics. Chi kung is practised by people from all walks of life and all ages. Early in the morning, you can see them gathered in any open space or even on the pavements, practising a wide variety of exercises. The young will do vigorous movements, while the elderly might choose more gentle, less demanding variations. It is estimated that around 70 per cent of urban Chinese do some kind of chi kung. It is also now firmly established here in the West, of course, and growing in popularity all the while.

Because of the venerable age and tradition of chi kung, however, it is fair to say that there are probably hundreds of different styles at large in the world today. And among these you will find all the many individual exercises and postures, breathing techniques and meditations that these styles contain. A set of encyclopaedias would not be enough to cover the half of it, let alone a small book of this kind. The same goes for the individual learning experience. You could spend a lifetime, all your waking hours of every day, trying to learn the different exercises and styles, and never really manage to assimilate more than a fraction of what is available.

Don't despair! Learning chi kung is not as daunting a prospect as it might seem – and for two very good reasons. First, there is a common thread, a shared *modus operandi* running through all chi kung practice, with many of the styles and individual exercises being in essence remarkably similar to one another. Secondly, as any good chi kung teacher would tell you, it is far better to apply your efforts to one small area of study, and to do it thoroughly, than to disperse your energies by constantly moving on from one method to the next and, as a consequence, probably getting nowhere.

Digging the well

A good analogy to this is the story of someone digging a well. What would you think was the best strategy if you lived in a remote rural community and were in need of water? This could be a life or death situation during a dry spell. So what would you do? Would you dig a hole for five minutes, give up and then move on and dig another hole somewhere else, leaving behind a pockmarked landscape of little dust holes behind you as you go? Or would it be better to consider carefully beforehand where the most likely place for water might be, perhaps take a little advice from someone on hand, too, and then dig – and keep on digging in the same place until you eventually hit water?

If you think the latter would be the best approach, great! You are going to enjoy this book. Because by repeating the exercises revealed here on a daily basis and keeping at it, steadily, you will achieve real and lasting results. The key to it all is practice – regular, daily practice. This is the most difficult thing about chi kung – the faith in the system. To 'keep on digging' and not become discouraged by the apparent simplicity of the exercises themselves and then move on to something else. Everything you will find in these pages shares a common origin with all chi kung practice – just as the well in our little story, shares a common source to all the rest of the water in the world. You are on target, therefore, and digging in the right place.

Welcome to the well!

Putting the *chi* into chi kung

Whatever chi kung you find is suitable for your needs, you will be applying yourself to one very important and central principle: the cultivation of internal energy or *chi*. But what is chi? And why is it so important for us? In order to go even some way towards answering these questions it is essential to realize that for the Chinese and other oriental cultures, even to this day, the physical world and, to a great extent, the emotional/mental world as well, is steeped in an environment of energy. Energy is considered to flow through all things and is shared by all things. The weather is attributed to the energy of the sky and the seasons; an earthquake is a disturbance in the energy of the ground; an unhappy home is a reflection of bad *feng shui* or poorly circulating energy. This is the chi in chi kung. It has numerous forms and characteristics that vary greatly, but in a general sense it is a universal substance, a universal energy present in all things.

In chi kung, when we talk of energy, we don't mean the kind of erratic, restless energy we experience when, say, we drink a cup of strong coffee. That's not energy, anyway, but merely stimulation. Rather, what we are talking about here is a subtle internal vitality that powers and nourishes all the life-support systems of the human body, everything from the circulation of blood to the fitness of our muscles, our tendons and internal organs. You can see chi in a person's eyes – that certain sparkle and *joie de vivre* when someone is in good health and full of enthusiasm for life. Children have it. Animals have it. People in love have it. We all have some – but we can lose it to a degree as we grow older or if we are unwell. One of the wonderful things about chi kung on a mental level is that it helps us rediscover that sparkle.

Chi – movement and measurement

All bodily processes rely on electrical impulses of one form or another, and the human body is no exception. It is a complex array of electrical fields and neural pathways. Sounds very complicated and scientific, perhaps, but the ancient Chinese knew of the existence of such fields, and they knew it thousands of years ago, long, long before the advent of our electrically driven age.

The *Jingluo*

Chi flows along certain pathways in the body – 12 of which are bilateral. These are the well-known acupuncture channels of oriental medicine (Figure 1). It is along these channels that the acupuncture points are mostly located, special places which are needled or massaged in clinical practice. In addition to these channels, however, there are what are know as the 'eight extraordinary vessels' – some of the earliest to be formed as the foetus begins to develop in the womb and which later continue to act as special reservoirs of energy in the adult body. Finally, there are also numerous minor branches and connecting pathways located all over the body, rather like the way blood vessels reach out to every part by branching out into smaller and smaller capillaries. Collectively, all these channels make up what is called the *Jingluo* – which means simply 'meridians and collaterals'.

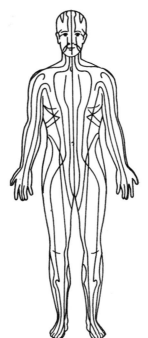

figure 1 chi flow diagram

When viewed as a whole, the *Jingluo* forms a continual pathway of energy circulating around the body. As it goes, the chi passes through the various internal organs in a constant and strictly defined sequence. And it is from these vital internal organs that the major acupuncture channels take their names. So, for instance, the channel that passes through the liver is called, not surprisingly, the Liver channel. That which passes through the stomach, the Stomach channel and so on. You don't need to know the location of all these channels in any detail for the purposes of the exercises shown in this book but, occasionally, you will be urged to visualize the energy flowing along certain approximate pathways: along the inside of the arms, for instance, or the outside of the legs. This enables us to take advantage of one very important law – that the mind moves the chi. Chi will flow far more efficiently whenever there is a certain degree of concentration or visualization involved. We incorporate this into our practice.

Here, then, is a list of the 12 major acu-channels, or meridians, along with the location of their superficial pathways. These pathways also exist deeper inside the body, by the way, and they have a surprisingly broad band of influence, affecting whole muscle groups and joints along the way. We classify these channels into pairs, usually, according to the Five Elements of oriental culture and philosophy. The elements – Wood, Fire, Earth, Metal and Water – are central to your understanding of the chi kung being described in this book, and we will have much to say about them later as we approach each exercise.

The Wood element
Gall bladder channel – eyes, head, neck, shoulders, flanks, hips, outer legs to fourth toe.

Liver channel – big toe, inside leg, abdomen to chest.

The Fire element
Heart channel – chest, inside of arms to little finger.

Small intestine channel – little finger, edge of arm, shoulder, neck to face.

The Fire element also has two extra channels:

Pericardium – chest, inside arm, palm to middle finger.

Triple Heater – fourth finger, outside arm, shoulder, neck to head and face.

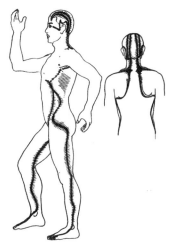

figure 2 Wood element

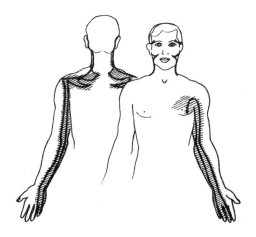

figure 3 Fire element

The Metal element (Figure 4)

Lung channel – chest, inside of arm to thumb.

Colon channel – index finger, edge of arm, throat to face.

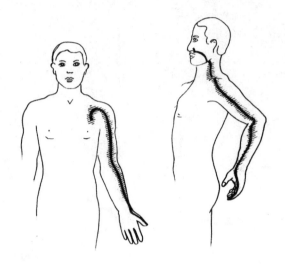

figure 4 Metal element

The Water element

Bladder channel – eyes, head, neck, back, back of legs to little toe.

Kidney channel – sole of foot, inside-back of legs, abdomen to chest.

The Earth element

Stomach channel – face, throat, chest, stomach, front of legs to second toe.

Spleen channel – big toe, inside of legs, stomach to chest.

Note: for purposes of clarity, the illustrations here (Figures 2–6) show the channels and the areas of their influence on one side of the body only. They are in fact bi-lateral.

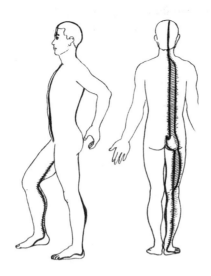

figure 5 Water element

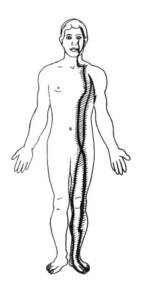

figure 6 Earth element

But are they real?

Do not ever be deceived into thinking that these energy fields or channels are imaginary items, something belonging to the realms of fantasy or ancient philosophy. They are used constantly every day in clinical practice the world over by thousands of skilled men and women working in the field of oriental medicine. They are, moreover, quite easily detectable through modern scientific instruments. If, for example, we measure the electrical resistance of the skin (that is, measure how easily electricity flows in any place on the surface of the body), we find all the traditional acupuncture points concentrated in small areas of particularly low resistance – remarkable enough as a fact on its own; but when we also discover that these areas, or points on the body lie in exactly the same places as depicted on the old drawings and charts of the Chinese physicians – some of which date back several centuries and are based on a knowledge dating back over 3000 years – we can justifiably be amazed! So yes, they *are* real.

Something in the air

So chi undoubtedly exists – you can measure its presence, even though you cannot see it. But can you sense it in any other way? Well, yes, you can. You can feel it in the air! Those who study the electrical energy of the atmosphere have established the existence of small, electrically charged particles called ions. These particles can be either positively or negatively charged and we find the negatively charged ones in places with fresh, moist, well-circulating air. Positive ions, by way of contrast, seem to accumulate in areas of pollution and dust. The uplifting energy we get from a walk by the sea is therefore all about the predominance not only of oxygen, but also the negative ions of the atmosphere found in abundance there. This is a very clear echo of our understanding of chi and is why those practising chi kung usually prefer to do so outdoors, early in the morning if possible in the moist fresh air near to trees or flowing water. This is where the chi has always been thought to predominate and now we can prove it!

Chi and health

Chi is what sustains us. In oriental medicine the diagnosis and treatment of illness relies on an intimate understanding of this most precious of substances, so that in therapies such as acupuncture or shiatsu the practitioner or doctor will be working around an energy-based theory of disease rather than a viral and bacterial one as we find in most Western medical practices. For a practitioner of oriental medicine, therefore, a blockage or disturbance in the flow of chi, depriving the vital organs of their natural power source, is considered paramount in the onset or progress of illnesses of almost every kind. A skilled practitioner will remove the blockages, redress the imbalance in a patient's chi flow and, so, ultimately allow the body to restore itself to a state of health, or even to go further, towards a condition of even greater health.

Beyond health

This is an exciting concept, and one which unfortunately is hardly recognized as being possible here in the West, that we can – once free of disease – extend our average state of health still further, towards a space in which we feel fortified and stronger than ever. Think about it for a moment. When we come into this world we are naturally flexible. As children we are upright and balanced. But as we grow older tensions begin to affect the body. Modern research into the ageing process clearly confirms that stress is a major cause of illness and physical deterioration because it wears down the body's resistance to disease. Stress constricts the circulation; the joints become tight; the spine loses its mobility; and the circulation of blood and vital fluids becomes inhibited through muscular tension. One of the aims of chi kung practice, therefore, is to slow down this tendency or even to reverse it. This is achieved by eliminating areas of stress and tension, energy blockages in the channels that feed the various muscles and tendons of the body, which in turn can cause disharmony in the organs through which they flow.

This wonderful form of preventive medicine is delivered, moreover, not through vigorous exercise, by rushing around endlessly, exhausting our energies, but by strengthening the body from the inside outwards, through slow, gentle movement combined with calm, regular breathing that leaves us feeling more energized afterwards than when we began. This, again, is often a difficult concept for us to grasp here in the West. People are conditioned to believe that if the heart is not pounding and there is no puffing and sweating when we exercise, that it cannot possibly be any good for us. 'No pain, no gain' is the current catch-phrase. Unfortunately this kind of exercise is extremely biased in one direction. It might well boost the cardiovascular system, heart and lungs – but at what cost to the rest of the body and to vital organs such as the kidneys! People can literally wear themselves out in their bid to 'keep fit'. The spinal problems and osteoarthritis suffered by sportsmen and women in their later years is a good example. Chi kung is different. With chi kung you exercise the cardiovascular system and the rest of the body in equal measure – without forcing anything. And it all hinges on that one amazing substance that flows through each and every one of us: chi.

Chi in action

One of the best ways in which to understand the concept of chi is to examine what it means to those who are in a sense 'born' to it and who act upon it as part of their daily lives. For this, we need to look a little more closely at oriental culture and the way in which chi has always been perceived by people living in the East.

The Chinese character for chi (Figure 7) is made up of two separate parts that suggest a substantial and an insubstantial nature combined. One part actually depicts the character for rice, or grain – so a *substantial* thing, something you can get your teeth into. The other part is the character for steam or vapour – an ethereal state, something in the air. Chi, therefore, is the vapour or energy belonging to substance. It can be contained within it but it is also independent of it and can be released from it. Rice and steam, moreover, do tend to give the impression of something that is cooking – something, therefore that provides us with nourishment and, ultimately, vitality and energy. In other words, *chi*. So now you know!

figure 7 the Chinese character for chi

How chi works

The classic texts of oriental medicine refer to six functions of chi as it works its subtle magic inside the human body. These aspects of chi are not only relevant for understanding human physiology but can also be applied equally well to the external world. So, for instance, you find the same terms being applied as much to the increasingly popular art of *feng shui*, that seeks to arrange our surroundings according to the laws and of chi flow, as you would in, say, the practice of acupuncture. So here is a list, for those of you who like lists, of what chi does:

- transforms
- transports
- holds
- raises
- protects
- warms

We need to look at each of these in detail to understand how chi can be both a substantial and an insubstantial force and how it can be at work not only inside the human body but externally, too.

Transforming

We require chi in order to transform the raw material, the air we breathe or the food we eat into something the body can make use of. Chi, therefore, has the power to change things. In this way the body can manufacture blood, bone marrow and fluids. It can renew its cells and grow bones, hair and teeth. This is the transforming power of chi. Perhaps the ultimate expression of this is the gestation and birth of a baby.

In an external sense, the transforming power of chi can be felt in the way we decorate our homes or work space – in, for example, the simple use of bright colours or flowers in an otherwise dark or neglected corner of a room. This produces the perception of a certain kind of positive energy to places that may otherwise have been dull and uninspiring, lifting our mood. This in turn affects the way other people perceive us and suddenly – hey presto! – our 'luck' seems to change.

Transporting

Chi moves things along – it transports oxygen and nutrients to the cells, and fluids to the skin surface. It provides power to the muscles and tendons of the body. Certain organs within the human body, moreover, have a bias for transporting chi into different areas or in particular directions. The Lungs, for instance, are said to transport chi downwards. When this fails to happen, the Lungs become congested and phlegmy.

In an external sense, you can see chi at work in the placement of objects and furnishings in a room. We all know how frustrating and limiting some interiors feel if they are overfurnished or if we cannot move freely through them. Likewise, if air cannot circulate easily we can sometimes feel dull or lethargic. Chi needs to move and we need to feel that we can move with it. When we feel confident of this, the mind becomes free and the creative process is set in motion, bringing opportunity and increased chances of success.

Holding

Chi holds things in place. The blood is held within the vessels by chi acting on the capillary walls. The energy of the bladder holds urine. The energy of the Lungs is said to hold not only air but also moisture. When the Lungs are weak, for example, the skin perspires excessively. Pregnancy, meanwhile, is sustained by chi holding the baby in the womb.

In an external sense, structures such as buildings are considered to have stability if they are well proportioned and rest on good foundations. This is thought to be a special kind of energy – Earth energy, strong, supportive and enduring. Walls hold things in place and concentrate energy inwards. But if there are too many doorways, or if the room is too large or has no partitioning, the people working inside feel restless and vulnerable. A good office or home, holds its chi and cherishes its occupants so that those working or living inside feel secure and calm.

Raising

Chi supports things and raises them up. Abundant chi results in a straight and erect spine and firm muscle tone. The organs are kept in place by the upward pressure of chi in the body. When this is lacking the skin and facial muscles will sag, the organs will prolapse and pregnancy might not be sustained. In oriental medicine the energy of the digestive system and the Kidneys are vital in this respect. Without strength in these areas, incontinence and impotence can arise. The body becomes feeble when it lacks 'rising' chi.

In an external sense, chi as it flows through the landscape works as a supportive medium, endowing places with a certain indefinable presence and strength. Mighty trees or their modern counterparts in architecture, columns, lend vigour and strength to external spaces. Meanwhile, structures that are placed on a slope, or atop flights of impressive steps, like a castle, a bank or a temple, have a natural upward flowing energy. They are 'supported' by the chi of the landscape.

Protecting

Chi strengthens the immune system of the body. It joins battle with external pathogenic factors (bacteria, viruses and so on) and destroys them. The battleground is a familiar one: the respiratory tract – nose, throat, lungs – places where we first have those early symptoms of infection and illness. The kind of energy that protects us in this fashion is called the *wei chi* and it is often compared to a defensive shield. Elsewhere, chi can help protect the body from blows and falls.

In an external sense, buildings are considered to be well positioned in the landscape if they are not overly exposed to the vagaries of the climate or to physical intrusion – if, for instance, they have higher ground behind them, such as a gently sloping hillside and preferably to the north. This gives the feeling of protection and safety for those living there. If you like things to be practical, you could say the building in question would be protected against the harsh north wind. So it makes sense in many respects.

Warming

Chi has a vital, warming quality. It circulates with the blood and also along the vital acu-channels of the body to reach every corner and extremity of the system, invigorating it and driving out cold. When this action of chi is weak, we can develop muscular pain and cramps. Also, numerous urinary problems and gynaecological complaints can result from a deficiency of 'warming' chi. Without it, cold and dampness can become lodged in the tissues.

In China it is considered propitious if a building faces south, the direction of the midday sun (in the northern hemisphere, that is). This quality of bright, warming energy is thought to permeate the whole house – not just with heat, but with good feelings as well. Conversely, buildings placed in the shadow of other much larger structures are felt to be unlucky. There is a feeling of gloom about any place that has the sunlight appropriated by other buildings in the vicinity.

I hope that this gives you a better understanding of what chi is and how it works? It doesn't matter if you can't get your head around every detail of what we have outlined already, only that you come away with a notion, a general sense of how chi manifests and how it can make you feel different. Feelings are important – because as you will discover as you begin to work on the exercises in this book, chi kung is as much about developing positive mental energy as it is about our internal physiology.

The polarity of chi – yin and yang

The next important aspect of chi we need to be aware of is polarity and that there is both a positive and a negative form of chi. We have already seen how the air can have positive or negative ionization. And of course, lightning is caused by a temporary imbalance in the polarity of electricity within the rain clouds. Scientific investigation has recently revealed that the subtle bio-magnetic and bio-electric fields in our bodies likewise have positive and negative charges associated with them – again, confirming what the Chinese physicians knew thousands of years ago. So it is a very real phenomenon we are talking about here. Without this polarity, moreover, chi would be very dull affair, without any movement or change. For it is precisely these qualities, movement and change, that distinguish life from death. When things are alive and thriving they are full of movement and change. When things become brittle and stiff, however, they begin to die.

This special kind of dynamism underpinning the life principle, the interplay of positive and negative, is called the yang and the yin. Together, they make up the famous tai chi symbol, more accurately called the *Tai Chi T'u* (Figure 8). Yang and yin are mused over and acted upon constantly by those of us practising the arts and healing occupations of the East. Be it oriental medicine, chi kung, feng shui, flower arranging, poetry, martial arts – all these subjects partake and make special use of the interrelationships of yang and yin. In a descriptive sense, yang is a light, active and external force that motivates and inspires us. Yin, meanwhile, is the opposite, a darker, passive, more mysterious energy that supports and nourishes from within. It is the interplay of these two energies that underlies all the glorious diversity and evolution that we see in the world around us. It is also why we classify the acu-channels in pairs – one yang and one yin organ belonging to each element, as we saw earlier (pages 9–12).

figure 8 the *Tai Chi T'u* symbol

At a very basic level, the Chinese character for yang means 'the sunny side of the hill' while that for yin describes 'the shady side of the hill'. This simple opposition of sunshine and shadow, however, is merely one very basic way of looking at yang and yin as the following table of correspondences will make clear.

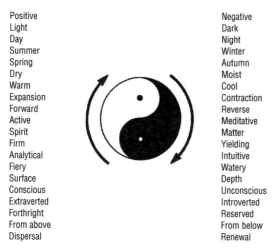

Positive	Negative
Light	Dark
Day	Night
Summer	Winter
Spring	Autumn
Dry	Moist
Warm	Cool
Expansion	Contraction
Forward	Reverse
Active	Meditative
Spirit	Matter
Firm	Yielding
Analytical	Intuitive
Fiery	Watery
Surface	Depth
Conscious	Unconscious
Extraverted	Introverted
Forthright	Reserved
From above	From below
Dispersal	Renewal

figure 9 attributes of yang and yin

It's always worth remembering, however, when looking at lists of this kind, that we are not simply considering opposing forces here. Rather, when dealing with yang and yin energies, everything becomes relative. A candle will be yang compared to the light emitted by a humble glow worm, for example; but it would become yin when compared to the brilliance of the sun. The key is simply to try to perceive a mutually supporting polarity in the world, rather than conflict.

In addition to being simply in opposition, therefore, yang and yin complement each other in many other ways and are described in the medical classics as being:

- Interdependent – that is, each relying on and supporting the other. Without an action (yang), for instance, there can be no reaction (yin). Often, too, it is only by reference to a point of stillness (yin) that we are ever conscious of motion (yang).
- Interconsuming – or drawing upon each other. Too much water (yin) puts out fire (yang). The food we eat nourishes our bodies (a yin function) by providing energy (yang). But at the same time we use energy (yang) in order to digest the nutrients (yin).
- Intertransforming – too much heat (yang) destroys fluids (yin) causing things to evaporate, leaving empty space (yin). Intense cold can also burn, of course.

A further glance at the *Tai Chi T'u* symbol confirms all of these points – and do take note, also, of the small seed embedded within each half, the white or black dot, indicating the potential for change and transformation at the heart of each phase of the circle – yang always ready to change to yin and vice versa.

Polarity and chi kung

The importance of yang and yin for those of us studying chi kung is that we work constantly with rhythm, not just the rhythm of physical movement but also the rhythm of the breath. The breath is a perfect example of the *Tai Chi T'u* in action. We use the alternating rhythm of the breath, in and out, to produce a dynamic sense of movement within the energy field of the body. In this context, the way we assign the in-breath and out-breath to yang or yin varies and can be used in different combinations, depending on our aims. In the exercises in this book, for example, the inhalation is considered an expression of yang energy; the exhalation as yin. But there are exceptions and in the martial arts this pairing is usually reversed – so the out-breath is yang. The main thing to remember here, is that as long as the breath is co-ordinated to the physical movements it will provide the key to much of the mental process underlying the exercises. With the breath, you become wholly engaged in the exercise, with everything working together in harmony.

This is a vital concept to grasp. In most of life we move and function in a fairly disjointed, haphazard fashion. Occasionally, we may manage to co-ordinate our actions with our breath, as in sports for example – something like tennis or golf. Or we may manage to get our thoughts in tune with our actions – as when concentrating on a meticulous task, painting a picture or threading a needle. But only rarely do we manage to bring body, mind and breath together. When we do, however, it can be a very powerful moment. In chi kung, we are trying to combine all three and, moreover, to sustain the combination for several minutes. This 'prime time' is of enormous value in terms of health and overall well-being and, with daily practice, extends its qualities outwards to every aspect of our lives.

This brings us nicely into the next chapter of this book, in which we look at exactly how we can prepare ourselves for this prime time and set up our daily plan of practice and study.

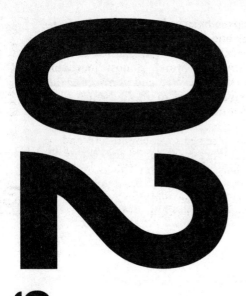

03

getting started

In this chapter you will learn:
- how chi can become 'stuck'
- how to warm up before your chi kung exercises
- why the breath is so important in chi kung.

In this chapter we will discover exactly how we can begin to harness our own vital energy and put it to work. One thing we have to bear in mind, however, is that chi kung is not an exact science. It relies, instead, on the natural, almost inevitable ability of the human body to regulate itself and promote health and vitality without effort. This it strives to do, of course, all of the time. Each human cell is a miracle of self-regulating energy, while the vast network of nerves, muscles, organs, bones and blood vessels of the body all manage to communicate and to maintain themselves in perfect working order 99 per cent of the time without any outside help whatsoever. Things only go wrong when disharmony arises. And how does disharmony arise? Well, that is a matter that we will certainly have to investigate. But stress and emotional tension are pretty high up on the list of suspects.

The emotional body

Emotions – major emotions such as anger, grief, joy or fear – are important for those of us studying chi kung because these feelings, in excess, can cause blockages in our chi flow and can, over time, quite literally make us ill! This concept may be difficult for many readers of this book to accept, since here in the West we like to think of the mind and body as being totally separate entities. The continuous interaction of mind and body, however, is very clear to those of us working in this field and is used daily in clinical practice. Emotions are part of the organs. They reside in them, they are affected greatly by them.

In these pages we will be placing great emphasis on transforming negative emotional energy into something more constructive. Preparing for practice, therefore, has as much to do with getting the feelings right, about mental focus and visualization as it does with posture. It is useful, therefore, to have some understanding of the way energy can work on the body and mind in equal measure and how it controls, and also is controlled by, the major emotions.

How chi can become stuck

As we have seen, from very early times it was known in China and other parts of the East that the human organism is sustained by a network of energy, or chi, and that this energy flows along certain pathways or channels. If the muscles and tissues through which any of these channels pass become tense or injured in any way, then the flow of chi can be impeded, leading to even more stiffness and discomfort. The origin of this problem might not necessarily lie at the site of the blockage itself, however, but within the organ through which the channel flows *and* its relative emotion. So, for instance, painful shoulders could be a result of injury to that area, or – more often than most people would probably suspect – be due to an imbalance in the Gall Bladder, the organ through which one of the channels that run through the shoulders passes. This, moreover, is a two-way process, so that blockages or weaknesses in the channels can also lead back to disharmony in the organs – in a way, more serious, of course. The Gall Bladder is greatly affected by emotions such as anger or frustration.

Vital organs – two by two

We also saw in the previous chapter how the vital organs of the body are classified according to the five elements and also in pairs, a yin and a yang organ that function together within each Element – for instance, the Liver (yin) and the Gall Bladder (yang). Each of these pairings are susceptible to and indeed some say actually controls a distinct emotional response. Here they are:

- Metal and the Lungs and Colon relate to the emotion of grief.
- Earth and the Spleen and Stomach relate to the emotion of worry.
- Fire and the Heart and Small Intestine relate to the emotion of joy.
- Water and the Kidneys and Bladder relate to the emotion of fear.
- Wood and the Liver and Gall Bladder relate to the emotion of anger.

Any imbalance of these emotions can have a profound effect on the relevant organ and, therefore, the channel that passes through that organ. Let's take an example: fear. If fear or anxiety are part of a person's emotional make-up, whether conscious or not, it will affect the Kidneys and Bladder and therefore the channels that pass through these organs. Some of the most important of these channels run along the back, sustaining and nourishing the muscles that support the spine. Weakness or tension in these channels can therefore lead to a weakness or tension in the back and, perhaps sooner rather than later, spinal distortion, consequent nerve compression, slipped disc and chronic pain. All from fear, and of a body which is not dealing with this emotion properly. Emotions are *powerful*.

The good news is that chi kung helps you become more aware of your emotional energy and therefore enables you to tackle these blockages directly through your daily plan of exercise. We will explore the consequences of blockages in these specific areas in much more detail in later chapters of this book. For the time being, we simply need to be aware of those parts where blockages can occur and try to make sure they feel relaxed and are moving freely as we set ourselves up for our practice session.

Places where chi can stick

There are several common areas in the human body where chi, for whatever reason, physical or emotional, can become stuck and blockages in the acu-channels can occur. These are:

- occiput (top of the neck)
- shoulders
- elbows
- wrists
- chest
- diaphragm
- lower back
- hips
- knees
- ankles.

A good chi kung teacher or practitioner of oriental medicine will identify where these blockages exist in their students or patients and will correct them, if possible. For the time being, however, you are going to have to rely on being very self-vigilant and honest with yourself. In other words, try to be aware just how the body feels, which joints seem stiff, which muscles are weak; which ones are tense and painful, and why. Maybe it is some habitual movement or position you have in your daily routine that is causing the problem – at work, for instance, the way you sit or even the way you sleep at night. Check it out! Maybe you need to change your chair or the position of your computer or TV screen. Maybe you are carrying bags awkwardly when you go shopping or straining muscles when you lift things in the garden. There could be a thousand reasons why some parts of the body seem stiff or painful, including emotional ones, but for now you can eliminate many of them simply through self-observation and common sense.

Putting it right

If you find these areas do not respond to your own best efforts, however, or to the normal cure-alls such as rest or the proverbial hot bath – then try any one, or more, of the following alternatives:

- Squeeze or tap very gently for a few moments on the area of stiffness. Then slowly stretch, without strain, or else gently rotate the joints and see if things feel any different. Tapping in this way is a time-honoured therapeutic device, called *do in* in Japan and which derives from traditional *taoyin* exercises of ancient China. See Chapter 09 for a more detailed explanation of this technique.
- Shake out – for example the arms – until they feel looser. In fact, to shake the body purposely, all of it – right up from the heels, through all of your body, then down your arms, as well, to your finger tips, has considerable benefits in its own right as a therapeutic exercise and is also a traditional chi kung technique. It frees off a lot of tension. Just a minute of this is sufficient, by the way.
- Get a good soothing massage, preferably from a qualified massage therapist or best of all a shiatsu practitioner. Shiatsu is a whole-body treatment developed in Japan which works on the energy channels as well as the muscles and joints, so it is highly effective for clearing away those blockages. It is also an excellent preventive therapy.

OK! Feeling all loose and comfortable? If you opted for the third choice, the answer is almost certainly yes. So now we are ready to look at the 'where and how' of our future chi kung practice. For this we need to pay special attention to the following factors:

- establishing a suitable environment and a time for practice
- warming up before practice
- checking posture and breathing at all times.

Time and place

Without doubt, the best places to do any kind of chi kung, even the following warm-up exercise, is outdoors. Remember, there is more chi available out there in the fresh air and it is at its most plentiful early in the morning, in the proximity of trees or running water. However, going outside to exercise will not always be possible for many people and should never be used as an excuse not to practise. Indoors is perfectly OK as long as the room is well ventilated and reasonably uncluttered. In other words, chi kung *anywhere* is far better than nowhere at all. The other essential feature of your practice area is that it is going to have to be somewhere where you will not be disturbed. This is because there is a strong element of concentration required in chi kung, especially at the start, when you are learning. If necessary explain to those you live with or share your work space with exactly what you are doing. Don't be mysterious about your chi kung and that way people will usually respect your wishes to be left alone for a while in order to concentrate and relax.

Cleanliness and a degree of tidiness are also important issues in any kind of interior space if it is to uplift the spirit and promote relaxation, and is especially important if you are to derive any real benefits from exercises such as chi kung. If you are indoors, make sure there are no artificial air fresheners or old, dusty pot puree in the vicinity, which are responsible for far more ill than good in health terms and also that there is a minimum of noise. And, of course, no smoke! If you are a smoker, then the message is a straightforward one: stop! You are simply wasting your time even contemplating something like chi kung, which places such emphasis on the function of the lungs, if you inhale smoke on a regular basis. This may sound harsh, but it is a simple fact of life. Smoking poisons the lungs and eventually the whole system. Kick the habit and take a more positive attitude towards yourself and your own health.

Clothing

For chi kung practice, your clothing should be of a loose, natural fibre such as cotton or silk. Wool is OK, too. Artificial fibres such as acrylic or nylon however, tend to store static electricity which interferes with your own subtle energy field and can be uncomfortable if you perspire. If you are lucky enough to be able to practise outdoors always make sure your kidneys and throat are protected, especially in the cold weather. This doesn't necessarily mean a great long scarf wrapped round your throat several times, but rather simply taking sensible precautions. And do always have something on your feet – socks at the very least if inside, or soft shoes preferably (but no high heels) when outside. Bare feet can absorb cold and damp from the environment – which, over time, is injurious to your health. So if you are outdoors, the footwear needs to be waterproof as well.

Warming up

Before any chi kung session it is always useful to warm up a little. If you are already into sports or do training of any kind you will probably have an idea already of what I mean. Rolling of the arms and shoulders, for instance, or touching of toes are both suitable exercises – but here are some other suggestions which are quick and easy and which, in just a couple of minutes, can loosen up most of the major joint groups of the body. One word of caution: if you have any chronic illnesses and especially if you have skeletal or arthritic disease, always check with your doctor before attempting any new exercise regime; and, in any event, always go through these movements slowly and without strain.

1 Standing with the feet apart, spaced at about the distance of one shoulder tip to another (to be known throughout this book as 'shoulder width'), bend the knees a little and relax. Raise the arms and rotate them, rolling forwards, alternating left and right, as if swimming in the air. Do this a few times, then reverse direction and, still swimming, make a kind of back-stroke movement with the arms – again several times. This loosens the shoulders nicely. But do watch out for low ceilings or beams!

2 Turn your head very slowly to look over your shoulder, then slowly back to turn the other way to look over your other shoulder. Not too far! Just gently. As you do this try to keep your shoulders and fingers relaxed. Keep the shoulders and the body still, as well. Just move the head, slowly. Repeat several times.

3 Hold out the hands in front of you, with the wrists loose and fingers pointing downwards. Rotate the hands, around and around for a few moments, then reverse direction and rotate again the other way, as many times as you like. Then shake out your hands vigorously, as if you have discovered a sticky toffee paper clinging to each finger. Let the shake develop right up to the elbows if possible. Shake until those wrists feel really loose!

By the way, try to make these rotational movements spherical in nature, rather than just flat, in other words moving up and down as well as simply around and around.

4 Set your feet wide apart, a little more than shoulder width if you can and then twist your body to one side, allowing your arms to flop around as you go, hanging loose. Then twist back and turn to the other side, the arms flopping round,

hanging loose like a rag doll. Then repeat, back and forth, turning from the waist and twisting from side to side. Once you are comfortable with this movement, extend the twist by momentarily raising the opposite heel to which you turn. So if you are twisting to the right, raise the left heel, and vice versa (Figure 10). Try to build up a little momentum with this movement if you can. It's important to keep the knees apart and bent, as if sitting on a horse, and also to keep the shoulders relaxed. The movement comes from the centre, from the waist – not from the shoulders and arms, which remain relaxed throughout.

figure 10 twisting exercise

5 Making sure you feel properly balanced, raise one foot and rotate it slowly, around and around in one direction, then change direction and rotate the other way – similar to the wrist exercise we've just done. Then gently shake the foot or make a series of rapid little kicks with the toes to loosen up the ankle still more. At first when you shake the foot, it may feel stiff, like a lump of concrete hanging their on the end of your leg; but with practise it starts to loosen up and feel good. Persevere!

Repeat with the other foot and shake out again in the same way. (If your balance is poor, use a wall or chair for support.)

6 With both feet close together, slowly bend the knees and squat down a little, then up again. Keep your heels flat on the ground as you go, then repeat several times, progressively loosening up the knee joint. All of chi kung is done with the knees bent and the weight low slung. So those knees need to feel comfortable and relaxed at all times. Don't squat down too far at first if you are stiff, and – again – if your balance is poor, use a chair or a wall for support. No disgrace in this. Make sure you feel safe at all times.

7 With the feet as wide apart as is comfortable, squat forward on one leg and gently allow the back leg to stretch a little. (Figure 11). Go very slowly with this one, then change sides and stretch the other leg. Experiment with different ways you can stretch different parts of the leg by varying the way you do this movement. However, make sure you do not push down on your thigh or knee with your hands at any point. It's OK to have the hands resting on the leg, but don't use this as a way of supporting your body weight. Rather, allow your weight to transfer down into the legs and feet. If you are properly balanced, this will happen naturally. Go slowly until you feel this is being achieved, and never, *never* strain or force yourself into a squat that feels awkward.

figure 11 leg stretch

Remember, this is not a gymnastic exercise, and you should never feel that you are stretching or straining in any sense. Some people will be quite supple, of course and almost able to get their bottom onto the ground as they stretch! Don't worry if you are not numbered among these paragons of flexibility. None of these dramatic gestures will make the slightest bit of difference to the circulation of chi that is the priority in chi kung practice. Just relax and be kind to yourself. Don't force anything, then it will all happen effortlessly.

Posture and breathing

Chi kung, and many of the other exercise systems of the East, such as tai chi, for instance, are distinguished by their low stance, a certain stealth-like aspect to the body, where the knees are bent, the centre of gravity low and the shoulders relaxed at all times. It should feel as if the feet are rooted in the ground, or attached by suction, the weight shifting gently from side to side whenever a foot needs to be lifted or moved. This, however, must not be achieved at the expense of posture – and the spine, for example, usually remains upright throughout.

Practise right now a simple upright posture! With the feet shoulder width apart, allow the arms to hang loose at your sides with a little space between your arms and your body. Bend your knees – rather like you are about to sit on a tall stool. This tends to bring the pelvis forward, straightening out the inward curve in the lower back. Relax the shoulders and 'sink down'.

Good! Everything you will learn in the next several chapters develops and grows out of this basic stance which we are going to continue to look at now in much more detail. So, at any time, if you ever feel that things are not quite working out the way you expected, always refer back to this chapter and check that you are doing things correctly. What follows are the golden rules of chi kung posture. Don't expect to achieve them all at once, but rather practise them regularly until you can slot into them naturally, without conscious effort.

1 Knees bent

With very few exceptions, the joints are usually kept loose in chi kung and the knees are almost always slightly bent. This gives a low-slung appearance to your stance which is entirely appropriate, no matter how odd it might feel. Chi flowing through the legs can easily become stuck in the joints. So bend those knees – and try to sense a springiness to your stance, as if the knees are acting as a kind of suspension system, shock absorbers, providing safety and comfort to the rest of your body.

As you bend the knees however, make sure they do not 'cave in' towards one another – a sort of knock-kneed look which is definitely counterproductive since it weakens your stance and, in time, will lead to knee pain. Some sophisticated chi kung exercises do actually make use of a momentary knock-kneed position in order to keep chi in. Personally, I have never enjoyed chi kung exercises that do this and have therefore not included any of these exercises in this book.

If you discover it is difficult to bend the knees, or to keep them bent for any length of time, there is almost certainly too much tension in the muscles of your legs. Try some gentle forward stretches or sitting on your heels – or else some massage from a qualified therapist to help loosen things up. Never force the knees into any position they are not comfortable with. It may take some days or even weeks before you become suitably flexible in this area. So, again, as always, be patient!

2 Spine upright

By 'upright', we mean not just straight without leaning to either side, but also perpendicular, like a plumb-line, hanging vertically as if suspended from above. In the classic texts this is often described as a 'golden thread' attached to the top of the head and stretching up to the sky – the neck and spine suspended, therefore, as if from above (Figure 12).

figure 12 posture

To help you achieve this, think of that tall stool again. Try to tuck in the bottom, as if about to sit on the stool, so that the tail bone area slides under and forward, taking out some of the usual pronounced lumbar curvature that most of us have and which is, of course, perfectly normal. If you can tuck the chin in slightly as well as the same time, you will also eliminate some of the curvature we all naturally have at neck level.

Neither of these alterations to our normal posture is easy at first and should never be forced. If you have someone you can call upon for help at this stage, all the better. Ask them to place the palm of their hand on your lower back and experiment until they confirm that you have managed to straighten it somewhat. Then ask them to place their palm lightly on the back of the neck. As you tuck in the chin, you should also be able to push out the back of the neck straighter and so your friend will feel this push against their palm and possibly sense the neck lengthening out slightly, as well. Don't expect major changes at first. Be gentle and patient at all times and gradually you will realize what is meant by an upright spine. This straightened aspect to the spine then becomes like the plumb-line, so that whichever way you move your body, forward or back or side to side, the spine will always be hanging perpendicular, as if from that golden thread above; not leaning forward; not leaning back.

3 Shoulders relaxed

The shoulders are a common area for tension to gather and for blockages in chi flow to occur. This prevents circulation to the neck and, ultimately, to the head and brain, leading to all manner of health problems. Try to relax your shoulders, so that they have a low, almost drooping appearance. Many people who lead stressful lives have shoulders up around their ears, so tense are they – something which can even prevent them from breathing properly! Even if you do manage to get them relaxed, it is easy to tense up again while you are concentrating on learning your chi kung. So keep tabs on those shoulders and, whenever you suspect they are rising or tensing up, let them go! Give the shoulders a roll again and shake out the hands.

Between the scapulae (shoulder blades) on the back is also an area where tension can accumulate. Often those people who believe that 'good posture' means a chin-up, shoulders-back position – military style – suffer from severe tension in the upper back as a result of habitual straining. In fact, there is nothing wrong with letting the shoulders go a little rounded, especially when you are doing chi kung. As long as you keep the spine upright, as discussed opposite, you will be fine, and the chi will flow more smoothly.

Try gripping the trapezius muscles on the top of your shoulder with one hand and squeeze several times. This helps to release tension. Then do it on the other side. Better still, get a friend to give them a squeeze for you, which is an infinitely more efficient way of massaging the muscles in that location – and very pleasant, too. And now you have a great excuse – it's all for the benefit of your chi kung!

4 Feet not too close together

In chi kung it is rare for the feet to be positioned closer to each other than the width of your shoulders – that is, the distance from one shoulder tip to the other. When the feet are placed in a position directly beneath the shoulders like this, the body can become what we call 'rooted' – that is, feeling well balanced. If the knees are bent as well, you can develop a very sound position indeed, which, over time, really can feel as if you have roots going down into the ground.

Some of the exercises in this book call for shoulder width, others for more than shoulder width. To a certain extent it all depends on how happy you feel about it. Those with some experience of dancing, or yoga, tai chi or martial arts will be confident with a wide stance. Those who may be elderly, in some way disabled or suffering from stiffness in the hips and knees, may need to be more moderate. But generally, shoulder width is a minimum distance for the feet to be apart.

The feet in most chi kung stances are also often parallel to each another. This is an important concept to grasp, because so often we tend to stand with the toes pointing outwards – which is perfectly natural and comfortable, of course. But in chi kung we try to introduce a shape to the legs which is rather arch-like – giving stability to the whole of the body and allowing the chi to flow more smoothly. This means feet parallel to one another – like standing with the feet on railway lines. Alternatively, think of a great building. Think of the body as a tower, the legs as the arch, and the feet as the foundations. This is a very strong structure in an architectural sense and is perfect for chi kung, too.

5 Chest open

With all this attention on getting the spine straight and the shoulders relaxed, it is very easy to slip into a sunken chest aspect. The chi of the lungs and heart reside in the chest and any inhibition to their flow is bad news. Instead, try to lift the neck and head – remember the golden thread? Here the golden thread is keeping the head off the chest, as well.

There is a wonderful acu-point located in the sternal notch – that is the little hollow at the base of the throat where your collar bones meet. Put your fingers in that area now. One of the names given to this place is 'Heaven's Chimney' and it is a very useful point for relieving phlegm and mucus anywhere in the respiratory system. Names of acu-points are often very instructive – and here we are being reminded of the importance of having the chimney unblocked, so that chi can rise upwards and the breathing become more efficient. Keep Heaven's Chimney open when you do your chi kung. Think of the neck lengthening, the shoulders dropping to create the space in the upper chest and throat area. Don't force it – just be aware of it and all will fit into place in time.

6 Elbows rounded

Elbows, like the knees, should have a soft, open aspect to them. In the exercises you are about to learn, whenever the arms are held out in front of you, as they often are, or whenever they rotate or circle in the air from place to place, try to make sure you do not lock the elbows or form them into sharp angles. There are just a few special places where we actually *do* lock the elbows, but only momentarily, and usually to create a stretch along certain tendons and muscle groups in the arms. Otherwise, the elbows are always relaxed, soft and rounded.

If you have tension in these places, try shaking out again and gently squeezing the triceps muscles just above and behind the elbows themselves. This may help. The most important thing about elbows, however, is that they are kept away from your sides! This is one of the most difficult things to grasp when learning chi kung. So often, tension and stress seem to draw the arms inwards close to the sides, as if protecting the body. This can come from emotional insecurity as well as physical tension, and its avoidance, in my view, is a way of overcoming many emotional difficulties and inhibitions. So keep those arms and elbows out!

Imagine, instead, that you have a rolled up blanket or pillow placed under each arm, between arm and body. As you move, keep that pillow in place and don't squeeze it. This cultivates a rounded aspect to the arms and enables the chi to flow more smoothly. Equally importantly, it frees off your rib cage, diaphragm and lungs so that you can breathe more easily, too. Try it: experiment for a moment by breathing deeply with your elbows touching your sides. Then bring them away from your sides and breathe again. Notice any difference? You should do. Your lungs are now breathing easily. It's a good feeling.

7 Discover your root

Chi kung provides us with the opportunity to develop our sense of balance and confidence. In this sense, we endeavour always to find our 'root', that is to make sure our contact to the ground is firm and reliable. In this way the body becomes properly aligned, allowing the muscles (including the many internal muscles that we are not even aware of) to be relaxed and the chi to flow more freely. It is surprising how much energy we use up in trying to compensate for a poorly balanced body.

Getting the stance right and the balance strong is called rooting. It almost feels like you have sprouted roots out of your feet and that these are going down into the ground. To help you with this, be aware of the way the feet make contact with the ground. There are actually nine points of contact between each foot and the ground. Many people find this surprising. But think about it. Take a look at your foot. There is the heel, that's a pretty obvious part of the foot to be in contact with the ground. Then there are also the large and the small balls of the foot, just at the base of the toes. That's two more. Then there are the toes themselves, five more. Finally, there is the outside edge of the foot, this also touches the ground in places. Nine in all.

Try to get all these places in contact; bend the knees and sink down. Find your root through your feet.

8 Breathe through the nose

Noses are wonderful things. Big or small, Roman or retroussé, they are miracles of efficiency. Together with the adjacent sinus cavities they filter the air as we breathe, clean it, warm it and moisten it before it enters our lungs. This enables the respiratory system to work more efficiently, and ultimately boosts our supply of oxygen and that all-important chi that we derive from the air.

Ideally, there should not be any sound heard from the respiratory tract, from the nose, mouth, throat or chest as you breathe. This means we should endeavour to keep the airways clear at all times. Noses are, of course, places that easily become blocked – and mucus is the culprit, as we all know whenever we catch a cold. But mucus is something that can be controlled through certain precautions, which we will look at later in those chapters dealing with health and diet. For now, make sure your nose is as clear as possible, so you can breathe through it easily, silently and without conscious effort.

One of the best ways to clear the nasal cavities comes from yogic practice – something called *netti*. Netti involves the placement of warm, slightly salty water into the nostrils and then simply allowing it to trickle through. Any surplus mucus is then simply cleared from the throat. This may sound utterly ghastly to many people, but is, in fact, not at all bad once you become used to it (so I am assured). But even on a more modest scale, we can all do something similar for ourselves every day without any great effort by simply snorting up a little warm water into our nostrils, alternately from side to side, as we wash. A little discomfort for a few seconds is infinitely better than going through the day with a blocked-up nose. Blocked sinuses cause pain and bad breath and they are particularly troublesome if you are wanting to do chi kung. So do try to keep the nose clear and breathe through it all the time, as nature intended, and not through the mouth at any stage.

9 Breathe from the diaphragm

Now we come to what is one of the most fundamental aspects of preparing for practice: breathing from the diaphragm.

As babies growing in the womb, we absorb all our nourishment and oxygen via the umbilical cord attached to our navel. When this cord is severed at birth we have to breathe for ourselves for the first time, which we do quite spontaneously by repeatedly contracting and relaxing the diaphragm – a dome-shaped muscle beneath the chest and above the navel. As we contract this muscle, it descends a little into the abdominal cavity, allowing the air pressure in our lungs to decrease – that is, to become lower than that of the air outside. The result is that, without effort, the air flows in (Figure 13a).

Moments later, when the body is ready to exhale, the diaphragm relaxes and rises up, applying gentle pressure to the lungs. The air pressure inside the lungs then increases compared with that of the air outside and the contents of the lungs flows out, along with any waste gases such as carbon dioxide. Again the process is perfectly easy and natural, without any conscious effort at all (Figure 13b).

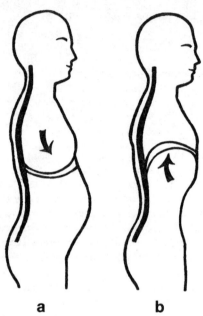

a   b

figure 13 movement of the diaphragm

If you observe young children or babies, or most animals for that matter, you will notice how the tummy area (just below the diaphragm) is always in motion with the breath – making way for the movement of the diaphragm, up and down. Babies have lots to teach us grown-ups, by the way. And they are certainly much smarter at breathing.

However, what happens as we get older is that we lose touch with this natural process. All the emotional tensions we become subject to start to interfere. Emotions easily go to the stomach and abdomen, as we all know. We can become nauseous, we can experience 'butterflies', or we can get bowel problems from the feelings that assail us. Over time, moreover, these tensions become stuck in the abdominal area, preventing the diaphragm from functioning properly. The result is that our breathing becomes restricted and shallow and that we compensate by employing the muscles of the chest and even, in some cases, the shoulders and throat to get the air that we so badly need in and out of the lungs. Breathing becomes laboured, strained and uses up large amounts of energy, resulting in an overall starvation of oxygen to the tissues of the body – not to mention the build up of toxic waste products in the lungs themselves which can, in turn, cause fatigue, skin complaints and even asthma.

And as if all this were not enough, there is also a centre of vital energy in the abdominal area, traditionally called the *tan tien* in oriental medical practice and in exercise systems like chi kung. This is a special place where chi is stored and where it can also be generated, as you will discover. It is vital therefore to breathe properly, and to relearn how to use the diaphragm if we want to make the most of our chi kung.

To get in touch with the process, try this simple exercise. Place one hand – say your left hand – gently against your lower left rib cage, just beneath the breast. Place the other hand, palm inward, just below your navel, or belly button. The thumb should just be resting in your navel as you do this – then you know the palm is in the right place for the purposes of this exercise. Before you start, however, please note that you must never, *never* force your breathing into any pattern that is uncomfortable for you. If you suffer from any kind of respiratory illness or heart problem, always check with your general medical practitioner before doing any breathing exercise.

Now, start by breathing in normally. (It is usually at this point, of course, where most students find themselves wondering just what 'normal' is.) Just do it, anyway, and see what is happening. If your left hand is moving and your right hand is not the chances are pretty high that you are not using your diaphragm properly. Try to relax the tummy, therefore. One way of removing tension is to lightly press with your finger tips beneath the diaphragm, that is, along and under the base of your ribs – very lightly, please! Then put your hands back where they were and try again.

Relax the shoulders and breathe in to your right palm again and try to keep the left hand from moving very much. In time – and this may take a while – you should be able to breathe in and feel only the right palm moving against your tummy, the left hand remaining still. Practise a little every day for a few minutes and it will come. Above all, don't force it! Don't thrust out your abdomen in an attempt to move the right palm. It must happen naturally, without effort; and the only way this will occur is if you can relax and disperse the tension in your abdomen.

Note that in some tai chi and chi kung practices that are oriented towards the martial arts, this method of breathing is reversed, with the abdomen contracting on the in-breath. This is not at all comfortable, but has its advantages. You may come across this one day but it is not, in my view, particularly helpful for developing calm and relaxation. Moreover, other teachers of tai chi who are more oriented to the health aspects of the art, follow the chi kung method outlined here (sometimes also called the Buddhist method, since it is closely related to meditation techniques).

Summary

So there you have it! It is not suggested that you try to breathe this way all the while or even try to breathe this way when you start to learn the chi kung exercises in the next few chapters. Just be aware of it, that's all. Practise a little each day and gradually it will become more and more comfortable and natural. Eventually you may find it is happening anyway, all by itself, even when you are not exercising. Spontaneity is the key to this kind of easy breathing, just like a baby!

And on that humbling note, we will close this chapter. I hope you will have absorbed at least a fair proportion of it before going on to attempt to learn the following exercises. Here, in brief are all of the points covered so far:

- Knees bent.
- Spine upright.
- Shoulders relaxed.
- Feet not too close together.
- Chest open.
- Elbows rounded.
- Find root.
- Breathe through nose.
- Use diaphragm.

Learn these well. Each one should, and indeed *must*, be carried through into your chi kung practice. Never lose sight of them. In chi kung, preparation is the greater part of learning, then practice takes over – and lots of it.

03

the big breath

In this chapter you will learn:
- a typical expansive chi kung exercise
- about the nature of the wood element
- how to nourish the joints and tendons.

Let's begin the first of our active chi kung exercises with the Big Breath. A wonderfully expansive sequence, this exercise illustrates perfectly the association between gentle movement and rhythmic breathing that typifies so many styles of therapeutic exercise. There are numerous variations on this kind of movement in existence – and these can be found not only in chi kung, but also in warm-up exercises associated with tai chi, the martial arts and hatha yoga. In a purely physical sense, the Big Breath provides us with some excellent, rotational stretches in the upper joints of the body. Mentally, too, it can be quite inspirational, as all of chi kung should be, of course.

Although, like most moving chi kung exercises, the sequence itself is quite short – just a few seconds in fact – it has been broken down here into five separate stages. Each stage represents perhaps only a second in time, but it is recommended that you study each one carefully and make sure you are comfortable with it before proceeding to the next. Be patient and soon you will be able to go through the whole sequence smoothly without any stops or pauses. You then repeat it as many times as you wish, of course, over and over.

Preparation

Begin in the neutral standing position as outlined in Chapter 02 with your feet a little more than shoulder width apart and parallel. Experienced practitioners can place the feet a little wider apart if they wish (Figure 14). You don't have to be too precise about this, in other words. Just find a comfortable distance for your feet, bend the knees, sink down and find your root.

figure 14 preparation

figure 15 lift hands

Directions

1

Begin by raising the hands, palms facing outwards, to a position just in front of your chest. The hands are fairly well spaced apart, the thumbs and fingers slightly separated from one another (Figure 15).

Tips

Keep your wrists loose as you raise your hands. Develop the movement gradually! Let it grow and shape itself slowly, without tension in the hands or fingers. If in doubt about whether the hands are relaxed or not, give them a good shake out and then try again until you do feel relaxed.

2

Continue by sliding the hands out to the sides in a graceful arc, to a position just above shoulder height and extended out from your body. Allow the wrists to rotate as you do this, so that the palms finish in a comfortable upward-facing position (Figure 16).

figure 16 arms outstretched

Tips

You can open up the chest and shoulder area by lifting the head and arching the spine back slightly as you separate the arms. Not too far! Don't let go of the bend in the knees, and always check that you are feeling properly balanced first.

This movement should extend the hands outwards as far as is comfortable without locking the elbows. By 'locking the elbow', we mean extending the arm out unnecessarily to its full length – which is not called for here at all and if done quickly tends to stop the energy flow anyway. So nice soft elbows please.

Keep the shoulders relaxed and loose, with plenty of space between your shoulder blades behind. And keep your knees bent, too, of course. In other words, don't launch yourself into this movement. This is chi kung, remember – not gymnastics. Be gentle and moderate at all times.

Note that the hands do not go overhead at any stage. Beginners often allow this to happen mistakenly, still thinking of gymnastics and the large, vigorous movements that typify most forms of exercise. Chi kung is not about large vigorous

figure 17 hands together

movement. So keep the hands below head level and that way the arms and shoulders will remain relaxed. You will also find that the hands make little half-circles as you go, like drawing half-moons in the sky.

3

Slowly slide the hands back inwards and together again in front of your chest, palms still upward facing for the moment. This is a horizontal movement of the forearms, across and inwards towards each other, not up and down (Figure 17).

Tips

With all this attention on the arms and chest, do not forget to keep the knees soft and the feet rooted to the ground. Make sure the edges of the feet do not rise up (see page 36).

Do not allow the hands to touch each other as they meet. This focus on controlling the movement and placement of the hands helps to develop a softness and lightness to your work.

Keep space under your armpits, too, as the hands are drawn in to each other. Elbows out. And imagine you have a large egg tucked under each armpit. Don't crush the eggs!

figure 18 lower palms

4

As the hands come closer together, rotate the wrists so that the palms are facing down and then lower them slowly, further down to the height of the lower abdomen (Figure 18). The hands are drawn in very slightly closer to the body prior to going down, the fingers pointing towards one another, but not touching.

Tips

As you lower your palms, you can bend the knees ever so slightly more if you wish. This gives a good sense of 'grounding' and is very relaxing and calming in nature. Don't overdo this, though. Remember, in chi kung the movements are usually moderate and never overstated.

5

When you are ready, slowly open up the hands again and draw them upwards until you find yourself in a position similar to just after the start, as in step 1 – with the palms now outward facing and preparing to separate out once again (Figure 19).

This constitutes one whole cycle and you can then continue on through as many times as you like, just repeating the movements

figure 19 lift hands

slowly over and over, from 1 through to 4, until, when you are ready to finish, you simply lower the arms down to your sides and stand quietly in your original position (Figure 20).

Tips

It may not seem that easy to make a smooth transition into each cycle. You might find that your hands come together, too close to each other as they rise and then you have to open them up suddenly to go into step 2, making for a jerky kind of movement. Don't worry. Very soon you will discover that your body is moving smoothly, with the hands and arms expanding and contracting smoothly in large, graceful curves as you sink down and rise up. Persevere.

Suggestions for breathing

Once you are familiar with the sequence, try to fit it around your natural rhythm of breathing. This means beginning the movement with the inhalation and then continue breathing in as you open up the arms. Then, when the next natural exhalation comes along, draw the arms back in again, rotate the palms and

figure 20 conclusion

lower them down to the level of the abdomen. Do this slowly, breathing out gradually. Then, with the next natural inhalation, lift the hands and open up again to commence the next cycle.

One whole cycle of movement, therefore, corresponds to one whole cycle of breath. So, like the movements themselves, try to keep this process even and smooth. This means inhaling and exhaling gradually. If you breathe in too quickly, you will have nowhere left to go with the breath. Same if you breathe out too quickly. Just relax and breathe evenly, smoothly and slowly, fitting the movements around your natural rhythm of breathing.

What you can expect to feel

This is an excellent, all-round exercise that works very gently on most of the major joint groups of the body. The wrists, elbows and shoulders get worked, but so also do the knees and hip area. Even the ankles and soles of the feet experience a degree of stimulation as the movement progresses. Because of this, you may experience some stiffness during the first few days as any energy blockages in those places attempt to disperse themselves.

If so, simply shake out, as described in Chapter 02 or gently massage the protesting areas until the discomfort disappears.

You should feel a warm glow of energy on the outside edges of the body, shoulders and legs as you work, as if your body were trying to expand outwards in all directions. Don't worry – it won't really make you bigger! But sometimes it just feels as if your are becoming larger, expanding your personal space around you as you work. For this reason it is useful to have plenty of actual physical space around you at the time of practice. And of course, in a very subtle sense you are growing with this movement, because the joints are becoming freer and more open all the while.

Mental focus – the Big Breath and the Wood element

As we have seen in Chapter 02 there are five elements in oriental culture and medicine and those acu-channels associated with the Wood element – the one we are particularly interested in here – tend to run laterally along the sides of the body, around the shoulders and the sides of the head (Figure 2). They also flow along the inside of the legs from the big toe up to the rib cage. So you can visualize this energy quite easily as you progress through the Big Breath. In terms of the seasons, Wood equates to spring – a time of growth and expansion in nature and of great outward and upward-thrusting energy. And the wide, expansive lateral movements here resonate perfectly with that kind of feeling. The spring and the Wood element are associated with those organs of the body (the Liver and Gall Bladder) that ensure a free-flow of chi to all the muscles and tendons and which also govern mobility of the joints generally. Because of this association with evolving and growing, Wood on a mental level also relates strongly to the process of decision making and to individual qualities of courage and self-assertion.

Vital substances – the Blood

Chinese medicine recognizes certain 'vital substances' within the body that are essential for life. Blood, perhaps not altogether surprisingly, is one of these vital substances and the Wood element and its organs are to a large extent responsible for its maintenance and its quality. In oriental medical practice, Blood is a concept which goes beyond the actual physical stuff that flows through our veins. As well as bringing oxygen and chi to all the cells of the body, it is involved with the whole process of moistening and nourishing – for example, the tendons, the joints, the nails and the eyes. In oriental medical practice, the Blood is said to be stored in the Liver – particularly when we are at rest, which is one of the reasons for this vital organ being associated with the Wood element.

The best way we can nourish the Blood is to eat lots of green leafy vegetables and also some meat. I suspect that those of you who are vegetarians will be happy reading about the green leafy vegetables, but perhaps not so keen on the meat! However, the quality of the Blood often suffers in those who pursue a strictly vegetarian or vegan diet – symptoms of Blood deficiency being tiredness, dizziness, dry or itchy eyes, weak tendons and nails, stiff joints, insomnia and forgetfulness. So nourish your Blood with good wholesome food, and allow your Wood element to thrive!

The General who Works out the Plans

In the classic medical text book, the *Nei Jing*, dating from the second century BCE, each of the organs of the body is awarded a descriptive title corresponding to one of the 12 principal officials at the Imperial Court. The court was seen as a perfect representation of the cosmos, and the officials who resided there, from the emperor downwards through the head of the armed forces, the civil servants and so on, all had their part to play in the great scheme of things, each one relying on and supporting the others. For the same reasons, the 'officials' also provided excellent metaphors for understanding the microcosm of the human body and how its various parts interact.

There are 12 officials in all, just as there are 12 major acupuncture channels passing through the organs. The Liver takes the appellation of the General who Works out the Plans. Meanwhile, the related yang organ, the Gall Bladder, is called the Decision Maker – responsible for what is just and exact. We are told that determination and decisiveness spring from the energy of this organ. In other words, organization and foresight, combined with the courage and conviction to put ideas into practice.

When the Liver and the Wood element are functioning well, therefore, we feel able to move forward and bring our plans to fruition. We can organize our lives and, with hope and optimism in equal measure, are able to fulfil our dreams and aspirations by responding to the 'blueprint' of who we really are. When out of balance, however, we can become disoriented and lacking in motivation. Unable to make decisions, we instead compose endless lists of tasks to perform, but never really get around to any of them. Life becomes frustrating and full of disappointments – largely of our own making. These feelings of frustration can form a vicious circle, moreover, further affecting the Wood organs and leading to even greater imbalance.

So try some positive mental focus – right now! Express yourself with the movement you have learned in this chapter. Think of evolution and change, of going forward with your life. Visualize a flower opening and closing as you go through each cycle – or if you are the more macho type, and not at all keen on flowers, think of the sea and a series of great powerful waves instead, rolling and breaking one after the other. The emphasis is on rhythm and gentle power, repeated slowly over and over again without stopping at any point. Constant movement is the way of nature, remember. Keep going – but slowly!

Let go of any feelings of anger or resentment, too. This is important, as Wood can lock these negative feelings inside us if it is not allowed to find expression. Leave all that stuff behind. This is *now* and *tomorrow* we are looking at here, not yesterday. Forget the past. Forgive if necessary, and move forward – thinking instead of outward expansion, optimism and personal evolution. Think of adventure. Think of growing and expanding with each cycle of movement, filling the space around you as you go – becoming stronger and more confident with each one.

Advanced practice

Once you feel comfortable with the whole sequence described in this chapter, pay some attention to the following points.

Try to slow the whole thing down! Breathe a little more slowly, a little more deeply, but take care not to strain or to feel uncomfortable. Try to grow into each part of the sequence, taking your time rather than rushing to get there. And keep moving. No stopping at places. No pauses. Just continuous movement, over and over.

Then, as you lower the palms, try to cultivate a feeling of sinking the body downwards. You can experiment with going into a shallow squat, but always do this with an upright body rather than bending forward too much from the waist or dropping the head. A gentle squat helps to stimulate the hip joints and the inner thighs, important areas where Wood energy can stagnate. There is something very tree-like about this kind of movement also, very much the Wood element again – first lifting energy up to the sky, drawing up from the roots, then bringing it down to earth again.

As the arms circle out to the sides, and as the wrists rotate to turn palms up (Figure 16), try to point backwards a little with the thumbs. Put a subtle stretch into the thumbs and energize them. A large area of the brain is responsible for the activity of the thumbs, so this is a useful exercise in terms of mental stimulation.

As we have seen, energy naturally flows around the body from channel to channel, organ to organ, and the energy of the Liver exits and joins that of the Lungs at the chest area. The action of the thumb here, therefore, helps facilitate this interchange – allowing any stagnant Liver energy to escape and flow onward to become good Lung energy. Mentally transform it – see it happening! Liver energy rising up and passing into the Lungs.

Finally, try to visualize the connection between the thumbs and the big toes. In chi kung we believe the thumbs and big toes are linked via the network of tendons. The Liver channel begins in the big toe; the Lung channel ends in the thumb. So there is a good feeling of connectivity about this entire exercise.

04

three burners

In this chapter you will learn:
- a chi kung exercise that uses increased mental focus
- about the nature of the fire element
- about the Shen – the vital spirit.

This elegant sequence is done several times to one side before changing over to do as many repetitions again on the other. It places special emphasis on harmonizing the activities of the internal organs and what in oriental medicine is termed the Triple Heater or 'Three Burning Spaces' of the body – an essential internal function that harmonizes the vital processes of respiration, digestion and elimination. The movements themselves are graceful and supple, like bamboo or reed swaying in the breeze, with the hand sweeping out and returning to centre three times before finally circling overhead and down again to the starting position – a movement that also benefits the shoulders and elbows greatly and stimulates the lymph drainage of those areas. There is more about the function of lymph drainage and why it is so important for our health, a little later in this chapter.

The sequence here is set out in nine separate stages. And, as we saw, in the previous chapter, make sure you are comfortable with each stage before adding the next. That way you will not become muddled or discouraged and it will all come together for you in no time. Then, once you have learned the sequence on one side and gone through it comfortably several times, simply transfer the whole thing to the other side and repeat. All this will become clear as you proceed.

Preparation

Begin in the neutral standing position as outlined in Chapter 02, but with the feet reasonably wide apart and parallel (Figure 21). The knees are bent, as always, like sitting on a horse. However, don't forget to keep the bottom tucked under as well – as described in Chapter 02.

Directions

1

Begin by sliding the right foot outwards and slightly forwards so the right foot is angled away from the parallel stance. You will find this helps take any pressure off the knee joint as you proceed. Then, shifting your weight slightly more into the right. Raise the right hand and extend it outwards and upward into the space above your right side, about the height of your shoulder (Figure 22). The left hand, meanwhile, remains relaxed, just in front of and slightly above your left hip.

figure 21 preparation

figure 22 open right hand to side

Tips

Make sure your knee remains above your foot as you swing outwards. This is very important. In fact it is so important, I'm going to repeat it straight away. *Make sure your knee remains above your foot!* Do not let it cave inwards. Or, to put it another way, as you look down at your right knee, it should be in a line of sight with your foot, so that the very tips of your toes are just disappearing beneath your knee. If you can somehow see your foot to the right of your knee, you must correct your stance immediately. Think of the right knee spiralling outwards in a clockwise direction – that will place it over your foot as you look down, and all will be well.

2

Continue by shifting your weight back in again towards the centre, so that your weight is again placed 50/50 in both feet. And as you do this, draw the right hand in towards the centre of your body, as well, down to the level of your left hand – or in other words the lower abdomen, right palm facing inwards (Figure 23).

figure 23 back to hand level

Tips

The level to which the right hand approaches the body is not critical. It should be low, but don't feel you have to bend, stretch or drop the shoulders in any way to achieve this. Be comfortable at all times.

Make sure the right hand does not touch the body at any stage. Keep the right elbow away from your sides, too. This ensures that the whole arm presents a graceful, curved aspect, with no sharp angles to inhibit the flow of chi.

3

Stretch the right hand outwards once more to the space at your right side, again about shoulder height – similar to step 1 (Figure 24).

Tips

Allow your body to sway gently to the side, with just the slightest twist to the waist as you go.

Without turning your head too much, try to follow the progress of your right hand with your eyes, looking at the palm.

figure 24 open hand to side again

4

Once again, shift your weight back towards the centre, so that your weight is again placed 50/50 in both feet. As you do this, draw the right hand back in again towards the centre of your body, but this time back a little higher than last time, to about the level of your left elbow, palm facing inwards as before (Figure 25).

Tips

As before, there should be no actual contact between your right hand and any part of your body.

Don't forget to keep those knees bent. Sink down.

5

For a third time, shift your weight slightly to the right once more and slide the right hand outwards and slightly upward into the space above your right side, about the height of your shoulder (Figure 26).

figure 25 back to elbow level

figure 26 open hand to side again

6

Again, shift your weight back towards the centre, so that your weight is again placed 50/50 in both feet. As you do this, draw the right hand back in again towards your body, but this time back even higher, across to about the level of your left shoulder (Figure 27).

7

Now things change dramatically. At this point, you roll your right hand up, back and over your head, palm up as you go. This should be a smooth movement flowing on from the last, so that after the right hand has drawn back to shoulder level, it then rotates, turns palm up and goes overhead, rather like an exaggerated 'brushing the hair' type of movement (Figure 28).

Tips

You will probably feel your hair against the back of your right hand as you do this manoeuvre. It does not always feel easy at first to rotate the wrist this much and provides quite a stretchy feeling to the outer edge of the forearm and hand, as well as the

figure 27 back to shoulder height

figure 28 hand overhead

inside of the elbow and shoulder. This, of course, is exactly what we are looking for! So allow yourself to focus on that sensation as you go.

Your weight distribution is slightly biased to the left side at this point – that is, just a little more weight in the left leg than the right.

8

Next, straighten out the arm completely, so it extends out to your side palm up (Figure 29). And slightly behind you.

Tips
Your weight distribution becomes slightly biased to the right side at this point – that is, more weight in the right leg than the left. So quite a lot of subtle shifting of weight is going on with these manoeuvres. Don't worry. Basically, it will all come naturally anyway, without too much conscious effort, the more you practise.

figure 29 arm outstretched

You can really go for a straight arm at this stage, by the way – albeit temporarily, as it is the stretching feeling in the elbow that we need to experience.

Make sure your fingers are not curled up in any sense. Stretch them too, and maintain that stretch.

9

The final stage of this sequence is simply to return your right hand to where it was at the start, that is fairly low down in front of you. Draw it back down and inwards slowly to the centre, beneath the navel (Figure 30). That completes one whole cycle, which you can repeat as many times as you wish, of course before drawing back the right foot to your parallel stance and preparing to change sides.

Suggestions for breathing

Once you feel confident with this sequence, try to shape it around your own natural rhythm of breathing. You may find this has started to happen already anyway because it is a very natural feeling to make expansive movements of the arms as you breathe in and to contract the arms towards the body as you breathe out. See if you have got it right.

So, in other words, always open up – that is, abducting the arm outwards – on the inhalation. Then as the natural exhalation comes along, draw it back in again, adducting the hand inwards towards the opposite hand/arm/shoulder. Then, as you bring your hand back in for the third time you should simply continue your exhalation as the arm swoops back overhead (Figure 28). Commence the next inhalation as you straighten out the arm (Figure 29). And then finally, when you are ready to exhale again, lower the arm and return to your starting position (Figure 30).

Directions for reversing the sequence to the left

To even things out, we must do the same sequence of movements to the other side, of course. So everything from step

figure 30 conclusion

1 through to step 9 is repeated just the same, except for 'right side' read left instead. To help you with this conversion, here are the instructions again, only in a very condensed from:

1 With inhalation, open up left hand to the left side, shoulder height.
2 With exhalation, draw left hand back in to level of right hand.
3 With inhalation, open up left hand to the left side again.
4 With exhalation, draw left hand back in to level of right elbow.
5 With inhalation, open up left hand to the left side for a third time.
6 With exhalation, draw left hand back in towards level of right shoulder.
7 Still with exhalation, swoop left hand overhead, palm up.
8 With inhalation, straighten left arm out to left side.
9 With subsequent exhalation, return left hand to centre.

What you can expect to feel

Because this movement works very much on the arms and shoulders, you can expect to feel increasing awareness of these areas and, at first perhaps, some stiffness associated with them, too. A lot of acu-channels pass through the shoulder area and this is a place that can easily become congested through stressful emotions. Any feelings of tightness, however, should pass after a few days of practise and you can, of course, help this on its way with some gentle tapping or massage as described in Chapter 02. After that, you can expect feelings of relaxation and calm to develop and a sensation of unity between all the different parts of the body.

People love this exercise because it gives them a very real sense of graceful movement. There is a wonderful flowing rhythm to it in which the whole body can participate. Plants such as bamboo (we can compare this to something like willow or reed here in the West) are pliant yet very strong. There should be feelings of lightness, therefore, with this movement, like swaying in the breeze, very flexible yet with strong roots. The area in front of the body feels very open, as if there is more space inside for the organs to function more efficiently, especially the heart and lungs.

This exercise, in particular, also stimulates the lymph nodes of the body, which are located in profusion in the areas of the neck, armpits and throat. Lymph is a fluid that cleanses and detoxifies the cells of the body and is a vitally important component of our immune system. The lymph nodes themselves are like tiny factories manufacturing antibodies and white blood cells to help us fight off infection – although most of us are only aware of them when they swell: a sure sign that the body's immune system is being mobilized. Lymph fluid itself, meanwhile, actually circulates everywhere through the body; but it has no pump, as the blood has with the heart, to move it around. Instead it relies to a large extent on physical movement. This is why tight, restricted shoulders and chests are so detrimental to our overall well-being and state of health and why exercises like chi kung are so beneficial.

Mental focus – Three Burners and the Fire element

In oriental culture and medicine, Fire is seen as the element that stimulates, warms and inspires. It is a creative, joyful element that, perhaps not surprisingly, is associated with summer. The acu-channels associated with the Fire element, four in all, are located in the centre and little-finger sides of the arms, flowing to and from the third, fourth and fifth fingers (Figure 3). The special chi kung sequence shown here naturally works on and stretches these channels, particularly during the overhead spiral and stretching out of the arm.

In the overall seasonal picture, summer is considered to be a time of growing and maturing, a time of colour and splendour when nature's energies circulate at their highest pitch. In the human body, the Fire element is associated with the circulation of Blood via the action of the Heart – an organ which can be thought of as the ruler of the fire element. The Blood is also supported by the Heart's coupled organ the Small Intestine where our food nutrients are absorbed via the intestinal wall into the blood stream. When these processes are functioning smoothly, we feel alert, energized and joyful. If not we can become nervous, depressed and forgetful. Physical symptoms range from palpitations and sleep disorders, to nutritional deficiency and fatigue.

The Office of Lord and Sovereign

Those acu-channels associated with the Fire element are the Heart, Small Intestine, Triple Burner and Pericardium, the most important of which is the Heart. The Heart has always been compared to the emperor in terms of the 12 officials spoken of in the *Nei Jing* – where it says 'the radiance of the spirit stems from it'. The 'spirit' in question is called the *Shen* – another one of the vital substances of oriental medical theory and said to reside in the Heart. Today, the *Shen* is assumed to embrace the concept of the mind as well as the more nebulous 'spirit' – and so embraces what we term the unconscious mind, as well. The *Shen*, therefore, motivates our feelings in a major way, often without our being aware of it.

When the Heart is functioning well, there is good cheer, warmth, sound sleep and mental clarity. The memory is good and the complexion healthy and radiant. We are able to respond to emotional warmth and love and we can share our feelings freely with others while at the same time recognizing appropriate boundaries.

The Separator of Pure from Impure

The Small Intestine energy, meanwhile, is particularly significant for those of us interested in diet and nutrition since it is called

'The Separator of Pure from Impure'. If the Small Intestine is functioning properly, we can eat most things and derive the goodness from it. In other words, we should not agonize too much over the odd gastronomic indiscretion if our Small Intestine is well. No harm should come from any kind of food unless it is manifestly poisoned. The pure and useful part will always be absorbed, the rest discarded, and food allergies and intolerances should be minimized.

The Official of Balance and Harmony

The Triple Burner is called 'The Official of Balance and Harmony'. It is not an organ, but rather an internal process that harmonizes and maintains equilibrium within the body. If you think about it for a moment, there are three major areas within the torso, each charged with responsibilities that differ markedly from the others. The upper segment in the chest, the Upper Burner, contains the lungs and heart, which maintain the circulation of oxygen and blood around the body. The Middle Burner contains the stomach and other digestive organs, that enable us to break down and absorb our food and fluids. While the Lower Burner is responsible for eliminating the waste via the bowels, kidneys and bladder. The classics describe this threefold arrangement, not altogether flatteringly, as 'a fine mist, a muddy pool and a drainage ditch', respectively.

If any one of these processes becomes weakened or else perhaps overactive, then illness can arise. The job of the Triple Heater, therefore, is to balance all three processes and to re-establish equilibrium. So as you go through this exercise, imagine you are doing just that – balancing each of the three burners in turn and bringing them all into harmony.

Advanced practice

Once you feel comfortable with the whole sequence, pay some attention to the following points.

With the overhead movement, touch the tip of your right index finger to the tip of your thumb and focus your attention into the stretch that is produced in the remaining third, fourth and fifth fingers as you go. Extend them outwards, nice and straight and go for a strong rolling and stretching sensation as you circle up, overhead and out. Let go of this thumb–index finger connection as you lower your arm to your side at the conclusion of each cycle.

Allow your whole body to sway as you open up and close each time. Most of us here in the West are not familiar with the sight of bamboo, so think, instead, of a young sapling such as willow or a tall reed swaying in the breeze. There is sunshine and shadow flickering as you go, this way and that. Your feet remain firmly rooted to the ground, but your whole body is in motion above these roots. Harmonize this swaying movement with your breathing until it almost feels as if the internal breath is like the breeze itself that moves the willow. The breath moves *you*, therefore, not the other way around. This is an important principle in all the moving chi kung routines you will find in this section of the book. All this will prompt you to calm things down, taking time to fashion each expansive movement slowly, then returning equally slowly to the start.

Mentally, too, try to cultivate a balanced and moderate emotional attitude. Think of the Heart being settled and tranquil, not prone to extremes of feeling, but simply calm and at peace.

Incidentally, in the arts and literature of the East, bamboo is seen as symbolizing youth and eternal life – a quality of flexibility that is somehow indestructible. No matter how often the bamboo is cut down or levelled by the wind, it somehow always manages to spring back or is regenerated from its roots. This idea has great lessons for us as we deal with the blows and misfortunes of life. Finally, remember, Fire is all about being joyful and happy. Try to cultivate this feeling throughout. Make a big circle with your hand overhead, like going around the brim of a big sombrero! The sun overhead. That's it.

05

drawing the bow

In this chapter you will learn:
- a dynamic chi kung exercise with concentration
- about the nature of the metal element
- more about the lungs and their function.

This exercise looks a little like an archer with a bow, drawing back the arrow and taking aim. It is based on a classic chi kung exercise, numbered among the traditional 'Eight Strands of Brocade' whose origins go back at least 800 years. Like the exercise we looked at in the last chapter it makes special use of the tendons of the arm in order to stimulate certain acu-channels. It is also another movement done on both sides. So once again, after you have learned the sequence thoroughly, simply transfer the whole thing to the other side and repeat. All this will become clear as you proceed and the instructions will, of course, help you with the transfer of sides.

The sequence itself is broken down into five stages. The feet play a significant part this time, as it incorporates a sideways stepping movement and then another sliding inwards movement at the end to bring you back to the original position. Make sure you are comfortable with how these sideways steps fit in with the arm movements and, later on, the breathing.

Preparation

Begin in the neutral standing position as outlined in Chapter 02, with your feet around shoulder width apart and parallel to each other (Figure 31). Experienced practitioners can start with the feet a little wider apart than this if they wish. Whatever the width of your stance, don't forget to bend those knees! Sink down and find your root.

figure 31 preparation

Directions

1

Pivot on your right heel a little to turn the toes slightly outwards from your parallel stance. Then slowly, shift your weight across into your right foot, to a proportion of roughly 70 per cent right, 30 per cent left. At the same time, begin to raise the hands, to about chest height. The palms face upwards initially, but will tend to naturally rotate inwards to face your chest as you go (Figure 32).

Tips

As you raise the hands, your fingers should be relaxed and loosely separated. Allow your right hand to be slightly further out from your body than your left.

figure 32 raise hands

2

Next, with your body still facing forwards, slide your left foot into a broad stance, up to twice shoulder width between the feet. At the same time, turn your head slightly to the right and

figure 33 extend right arm

extend the right arm out from your side. The arm becomes purely horizontal, in a line with your shoulders, but with the index finger of the hand pointing directly upwards to the sky (or as near directly upwards as you can manage). Allow your weight to settle more into your left side (Figure 33) and draw back your left hand across your chest to a position just in front of your left shoulder – pulling an imaginary bowstring as you continue to focus your gaze and your attention on your right index finger.

Tips
The straightening of the arm will result in the sensation of a 'tug' or stretching feeling in the tendon that links your index finger to the rest of your arm. This is perfectly all right.

Keep the index finger pointing skywards. Beginners tend to either lack the flexibility to do this, and so settle for a less erect finger, or else they become worried by the sensation they feel in the tendon as the arm straightens – so they let go of the tension completely! You should really endeavour to feel that stimulation of the tendon and in the finger especially. That's what this exercise is all about. Go for it!

3

Maintaining your position, and without any further physical movement, pause for a moment, focusing on the feelings in your arm, maintaining the pleasant sensation of energy in the index finger and thumb throughout.

Tips

During this pause, allow your gaze to look out beyond your finger to an imaginary distant horizon. Take aim – as if you were drawing a real arrow. This helps to extend your energy and encourages the mental focus you are seeking to develop (see the special section on mental focus later in this chapter).

Keep the left hand relaxed. Although the image is of drawing a bow, there should be no muscular, pulling sensation in your left arm. The attention remains on the right hand.

4

Now let go of the 'tension' in the right finger and arm. Let go of the bowstring also in your left hand and shift your weight across more into your right side. Allow the left hand to circle out a little to your side, so that the hands tend to be equidistant from your body. Drop your elbows (Figure 34). The head turns to face forward once again.

figure 34 open up

Tips

Make sure your shoulders stay relaxed throughout this movement. Don't raise them up or pull them back unnecessarily.

5

Finally, draw your left foot back in towards your right foot once more to settle in the starting position – that is, with the feet shoulder width apart again and parallel. The hands, meanwhile, circle downwards, back down to where they were at the start, in preparation for reversing the whole routine to the other side (Figure 35).

figure 35 conclusion

Suggestions for breathing

As always, begin the movement on your inhalation, raising the hands in readiness. Then with the subsequent exhalation, slide the left foot along and extend the right arm, drawing the bow.

As you maintain this position take at least one whole breath, in and out. Then, with the next convenient inhalation, prepare to conclude the sequence by relaxing and dropping the elbows. Finally, slide your foot back into its starting position and settle the weight 50/50 once more with the subsequent exhalation.

Directions for reversing the sequence to the left

To even things out, we need to do this sequence to the left as well. Because this is a particularly dynamic exercise, it is best simply to go through one cycle to the right and then alternate straight away to the left, then back again, and so on, rather than do several on one side at a time (as we did in the previous exercise in Chapter 04).

To help you with this conversion, here are the instructions again, only in a very condensed from. Everything from step 1 through to step 5 is just the same, except for 'right side' read 'left' instead:

1 With inhalation, pivot on left heel, raise hands, then shift weight to the left.
2 With exhalation, slide right foot along to the side, extend left arm, index finger upward facing. Right hand holds the bowstring. Weight shifts right.
3 Maintaining the position, breathe in and out, one whole cycle of breath.
4 With the next inhalation let go of bow, open hands.
5 With subsequent exhalation draw right foot back to starting position, drop hands and relax.

What you can expect to feel

Generally, this movement promotes feelings of confidence, a sense of inner strength, a particularly dynamic sensation both physically and mentally. The tendon that reaches to the index finger is very obviously where the attention lies. This is good. The whole of the arm becomes energized, possibly feeling warm and tingly as the acu-channels that run along the thumb side of the arm, namely those of the Lungs and Colon, become stimulated (Figure 4).

Generally, therefore, the chest and respiratory function should feel stronger with this movement, especially with daily practise; and the face can also feel strangely energized, as if the skin were being replenished. With time, you might also begin to notice an overall improvement in the functioning of your digestive system and, in particular, the bowels.

Mental focus – Drawing the Bow and the Metal element

The acu-channels that run along the thumb side of the arms belong to the Metal element in oriental medicine and they relate to what is often called the *wei chi* or 'the defensive shield' of the body. As such, this element has a very modern counterpart in the concept of the immune system. It is the *wei chi*'s defensive mechanism that protects us from external pathogenic factors and extremes of climate such as wind, cold or damp. When the *wei chi* is strong we can be exposed to any number of viruses or bacteria, yet most of these will not be able to penetrate beyond this tough outer layer.

Those organs associated with the Metal element and the *wei chi* are the Colon and, most crucially, the Lungs. Indeed the whole of the respiratory tract can be seen as an active interface between the internal and external worlds, between what is inside us and what is outside. It is where the battle between our defences and any invading pathogen usually takes place. And, as we all know, the symptoms of the battle are sometimes unpleasant – runny nose, shivers, headaches, fever and so on. However, if we are patient and do not dive immediately into the medicine cabinet for drugs that suppress these symptoms, the *wei chi* will invariably win the battle and the illness will be vanquished. This is the *wei chi* in action. But it has to be robust and strong in order to do the job.

In the seasonal cycle, Metal relates to autumn and, as such, it has always been associated with the notion of things passing, of 'letting go'. The other organ supported by the Metal element, the Colon, is, like the Lungs, also an organ of elimination, ridding the body of toxins and waste. Inside the body, deep channel pathways link the Lungs to the Colon, and the Lungs constantly send vital energy down to the Colon to assist it in its activities. This process of letting go of waste material, be it carbon dioxide in the lungs or waste matter in the colon, is essential for any healthy organism. We can literally poison ourselves if our bowels and lungs are sluggish.

The Minister and Chancellor

The Lungs, according to the ancient classics, are 'The Receiver of Chi from the Heavens'. By heaven is meant everything around and above us – so the air that we breathe and the chi that it contains. The Lungs are, naturally, the organ of reception of chi from the air and so the rather politically sounding title of 'Minister and Chancellor' refers to the distribution of riches, or of the chi, by the Lungs, to the rest of the body. The classic of oriental medicine, the *Su Wen*, says of this official that 'the regulation of the life-giving network stems from it.' This is a very clear reference to the distribution of chi, the major source of which is the air that we breathe. In a more scientific sense, we can say that the oxygen of the air is distributed by the lungs all over the body via the bloodstream and the chemical haemo-globin, which picks up oxygen from the lungs as the blood passes through.

Most types of exercise that people are familiar with in the West focus on vigorous rapid movements in order to increase cardiovascular activity and dilate the blood vessels. Chi kung, in contrast, relies on relaxation to achieve the dilation of the capillaries and therefore to transport more oxygenated blood to the cells. Its results are much the same as with vigorous exercise – but without as much effort or loss of energy. This is why chi kung is traditionally considered to be so beneficial for those with high blood pressure or those recovering from heart disease – while the very method of chi kung itself, with its emphasis on slow, gentle movement and breathing, produces feelings of calm which in turn can help regulate the circulation even further. So once again, when looking at the ancient Chinese culture, we see how well the physicians of those times understood, simply through careful and intelligent observation of nature, how some of the most intricate features of our internal physiology really do work.

So much for the Lungs. But what about its coupled yang organ, the Colon?

The Drainer of the Dregs

Regarding the Colon and the ancient classics, the *Nei Jing* awards this vital part of our anatomy with the not particularly prestigious title of 'The Drainer of the Dregs'. This is a useful self-explanatory term, however, since as we all know the Colon is responsible for eliminating waste matter from the body, the 'dregs' left over from the digestive process – but no less important because of this humble role. Consequently, constipation is always a bad position to be in because, apart from the obvious discomfort it causes us, it signifies a considerable waste of energy fighting off the consequences of our own internal pollution. The exercise shown in this chapter can assist the action of the Colon, helping to keep the body clean and working smoothly inside, all the better for applying those precious energies to maintaining a strong and robust immune system instead.

We saw briefly in Chapter 02 how the predominant emotion associated with the Metal element is sadness or grief. If Metal is disturbed or weakened, we may find it difficult to accept change in our lives, to let go of people and places, objects and ideas. This inability to let go of the past leads to stagnation and ultimately to physical weakness and disease which can be reflected every bit as much in our mental capacity for change as in the functioning of the bowels. Of course, it is natural and healthy to feel grief at times, when we lose someone or something which has been precious to us. But a persistently sorrowful, grieving person will eventually lose energy from the chest and bowel, and all manner of illnesses – from asthma to chronic constipation – can arise if this state continues for any length of time. Morbidity and sentimentality take the place of optimism and forward-thinking. It is vital, therefore, not to dwell on sadness but rather to transform such feelings into positive energy at every available opportunity.

Chi kung, of course, provides us with a wonderful opportunity to do just that, to alter these negative emotions. So with this exercise, open up and let go of any sadnesses. Allow any feelings of regret or any inhibitions you may have developed over time to become transformed into optimism and pure upright, defensive energy. See yourself as strong and powerful like a warrior drawing his bow in battle. Be bold and liberated inside, and with each breath visualize a brilliant white light surrounding your upper body. This is the defensive shield, the *wei chi*.

Chapter 10 deals in more depth with transforming negative emotional energy. But for the time being, just keep on doing this wonderful liberating exercise. Let go of all negativity as you work. You will feel marvellous if you give it a try!

Advanced practice

Once you feel comfortable with the whole sequence, and can perform it happily on both sides, alternating left to right, pay some attention to the following points.

During step 1, and even at this early stage of the sequence, you can start to shape up the hands in preparation for what is to come. If you are going to work on the right side, begin to think in terms of holding the bowstring with the fingers and thumb of your left hand as it rises. Focus your attention in the index finger of the right hand, too, as it rises – as this is to become the 'arrow head', of course, in the next stage of the movement. The right hand can also rise slightly right of centre. All this will develop naturally the more familiar you become with the whole cycle.

At the top of the movement (Figure 33), think of applying mental pressure to the bow, so that the right hand is almost pushing against the tightened bow itself. Put energy into the right palm every bit as much as into the index finger and thumb. But resist any temptation to tense up or raise the shoulders. This exercise, perhaps more than any other shown in this book, has the tendency to make you want to lift the shoulders un-necessarily. Be aware of this tendency and keep the shoulders relaxed as much as possible throughout the entire sequence.

A particularly interesting variation on the whole movement is to twist the body around a little to the side once the bow has been drawn. This can occur during the pause in movement, at step 3 in the instruction section. Gently twist around to the side and raise the leading arm, as if preparing to fire upwards, slightly behind your body and into the sky, likened in some traditions to 'Taking Aim at the Moon'. This is done on the inhalation and it should be a very mild twist only, keeping the arms and body in alignment throughout. Then, as you exhale, gently rotate the body back to its forward-facing position and relax before going into steps 4 and 5 to conclude. And remember – not too far. Keep everything relaxed throughout: shoulders, arms, neck – everything. Only the index finger and its tendon will experience that moment of pleasing stimulation.

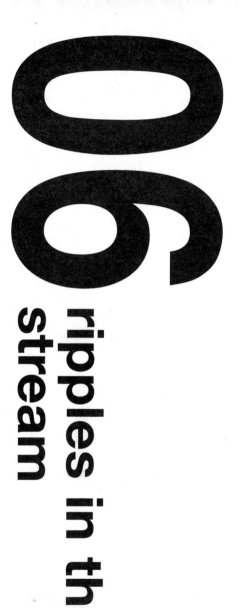

06 ripples in the stream

In this chapter you will learn:
- a rotational, rocking style of chi kung exercise
- about the nature of the water element
- about the Jing, the finite life-force within.

This is one of the most pleasant and relaxing of all chi kung exercises and comes from a set of very ancient movements sometimes referred to as *tai chi chih* – or 'Tai Chi Ruler'. The origins of these exercises dates back to at least the tenth century and it is probably fair to say that we in the West are fortunate to have them at all, because apparently they were once kept as a closely guarded secret within the Imperial Court and only came to the attention of a wider audience around a century ago.

The movements themselves have a wonderfully rhythmic, circular quality to them, like waves or ripples on a pond. They are done on both sides but, unlike those we have looked at so far, here for the first time the feet play a major role in establishing the pace and quality of the movements themselves, stimulating the flow of energy along the back of the body and back of the legs – again, something we have not met with to any great extent so far. This is achieved through a gentle rocking movement, back and forth. Soldiers on watch, compelled to stand for considerable lengths of time, know all about the benefits of rocking slightly on the feet to keep the circulation going. The powerful calf muscles in the back of our legs are sometimes described as 'the second heart' since they play such a vital part in helping to pump venous blood back up the legs against the pull of gravity.

The sequence you are about to learn has been broken down into just two separate stages, preceded by a lengthy preparation section. This is because the knack of learning this exercise is really all in the preparation, the movements themselves being very simple. So quite a few points to take care of first before we begin with the directions proper.

Preparation

From your neutral stance as outlined in Chapter 02 and with which you should be well familiar by now, slide your right foot forward and outwards. Your stance becomes rather like having your feet on opposite corners of a square, nicely spaced apart and with the front foot pointing out at a comfortable angle (Figure 36) Think of the sides of the square as being the width of your shoulders. This provides plenty of stability. Experiment for a moment and feel how the weight can be shifted easily from one foot to the other. Make sure it feels right for you.

figure 36 position of feet

Next, start to rock, gently forward and back. Do this by raising alternately the back heel, which will take you slightly forward, and then the front toes, to take you slightly back. Keep rocking, back and forth, with the spine straight. Try not to launch yourself into it. Keep the knees bent and the weight set low all the while. As you raise the back heel, the front foot will be flat on the ground. Similarly, as you raise the front toes, the back foot goes flat on the ground. All this encourages a stable yet flowing and variable stance.

Next, let you hands settle in a position just in front of your navel, with the fingers separated, the wrists relaxed and the palms facing downwards. Imagine your palms and fingers are curved around the upper surface of a large ball.

Observe how, as you rock your weight forward into the right foot, the hands will automatically shift slightly to your right. Conversely, as you rock back onto your rear foot, the hands will move in an arc over and back to your left. The result is that the hands appear to make a subtle counterclockwise circular movement as you go – forward and out to the right; back and inwards to the left. Allow this counterclockwise movement of the hands to assert itself a little more obviously by moving the arms very slightly and there you have it! This is the essence of the whole exercise. And the directions that follow, therefore, are really very straightforward indeed.

As the breathing is particularly easy to fit around the movements in this exercise, the suggestions for inhaling/exhaling are given with the movements themselves. Basically, it's all down to raising the back heel on the in-breath, then sinking back and raising the front toes on the out-breath. Here's how.

Directions (and breathing)

1

With the right foot ahead of your left in a comfortable stance and with your hands on top of an imaginary ball, wait for the next natural inhalation and then raise the back heel very slightly, rocking around 70 per cent of your weight forward into your right foot (Figure 37).

Tips
Note how the wrists and fingers have a very loose, almost 'dangling' aspect to them, remaining soft and relaxed throughout. However, do also make sure they have 'shape'. Continue to imagine them resting over the spherical surface of a large ball.

figure 37 left heel rises

2

As the next natural exhalation comes along, sink back into the rear foot by raising the right toes a little and putting around 70 per cent of your weight back into the left foot. The hands remain in the same position, but will rotate slightly to the left with the movement of your body, completing a counterclockwise circle (Figure 38).

Tips

Make sure the hands move continually in a horizontal plane – not up and down. Just circular, round and round with each repetition of this movement, the hands always resting on the ball. Alternatively, think of a large platter resting on a tabletop. The fingers circle around the platter, horizontal all the while.

As you sit back into the rear foot and raise the front toes make sure the right knee does not lock. In other words don't make this movement too large. Just a slight raising of the toes, not so high that your knee springs back into a locked position. Remember, the knees are kept soft at all times.

figure 38 right toe rises

This completes one whole round, like drawing one whole ripple in the stream. Then, as the next natural inhalation comes along, raise the back heel and go into step 1 again, then on into step 2 – another ripple in the stream – repeating the whole cycle as many times as you wish, only making sure your movements are co-ordinated with your breathing all the while; forwards as you breathe in, back again as you breathe out. Everything should feel entirely natural, never forced or strained. All chi kung should be like this, of course – but here the principle is very clearly set out. Breathe first, then move to the breath. Simple as that.

Directions for reversing the sequence to the left

You will find that you want to do quite a number of repetitions here as the cycle itself is very short indeed. But after you have done a minute or two of movement to the right, it is time to change over and do roughly the same amount on the other side, to the left – so that all the instructions presented above are reversed. For 'right side' read 'left' instead, and so on. The circle made by your hands will naturally change as well to become clockwise in direction, this time. To help you with this conversion, here are the instructions again, only in a very condensed form:

1 Place left foot forward and raise hands to about abdomen height. On the inhalation raise right heel and rock slightly forward (70 per cent of weight in left foot), allowing hands to circle forward and out to left side.
2 On subsequent exhalation, sit back slowly into rear foot (70 per cent therefore in right foot) and raise the front toes. Allow the hands to circle back in a clockwise direction to the centre, completing one whole round.

Continue in this way as long as you wish, completing roughly the same number of cycles as you did on the right side earlier. I should mention here that purists of this art would insist that you do precisely the same number of cycles left and right and may even urge you to count out an exact number of repetitions. This is OK, of course, but it does tend to interfere with the relaxing, meditative quality of the exercise and can turn the whole thing into a task rather than a pleasure. This, to my way of thinking at least, is counterproductive. Just do what comes naturally and enjoy it.

What you can expect to feel

This is one of the most calming and 'grounding' of all chi kung routines. The synchronization of breathing, conscious thought and movement, engenders an exceptionally peaceful feeling once you can relax into it without effort. In chi kung and other related disciplines we say that the breath controls the mind. And because the cycle of movement is shaped around the natural rhythm of your breathing, the whole routine becomes particularly satisfying on a mental/emotional level.

The arms sometimes become tired at first, perhaps even after a few seconds if you are not used to holding them in this kind of position. If so, simply shake out or massage gently, following the suggestions for dealing with energy blockages outlined in Chapter 02. As you work, your feet, ankles and legs may become warm or, alternatively, may feel slightly heavy, as if you have lead in your boots. The soles of the feet, too, might feel particularly energized and alive with the rocking movement, as if drawing up energy from the ground. People also sometimes experience a warm glow in the small of the back, the kidney area. That's good.

The motion of the feet is interesting here. Rocking is considered to be an energizing activity in the East and there are many chi kung exercises that avail themselves of this simple yet highly effective therapeutic device. Alternate rocking, moreover, also works gently and repetitively on those acu-channels that pass through the soles of the feet and ankles and which, in turn, generate movement and energy through the back of the legs and the back of the entire body. These are the acu-channels of the Kidney and Bladder (Figure 5), which – perhaps not surprisingly, considering the functions these organs perform for us – belong to the Water element in oriental culture and philosophy.

Mental focus – Ripples in the Stream and the Water element

The Water element relates to the season of winter – a time of stillness and hibernation in nature, but also one of storage and the condensing of energy into those tiny, all-powerful seeds, ready for spring. In the human body, the Water element is represented and ruled by those organs that have always been associated with vigour and hidden strength in oriental medical theory, namely the Kidneys. And if we bear in mind the close proximity of these vital organs to the adrenal glands in the human body, which produce chemicals to give us speed of reaction and impetus at times of physical danger or stress, it seems that, yet again, the ancient physicians had it right. The language may be different from that used in modern medical science, but the lessons are the same and the wisdom every bit as sound.

In fact, the ancient Chinese thought of the Kidneys as the very source of life. The reason for all this astonishing physical potential in such a small area is that the Kidneys are not only considered to be the foundation of the yin and yang of the entire body but also the source of a very precious substance. This substance or special energy is called the *Jing*. The *Jing* was seen to have a very close relationship with the growth, development and the ageing process, along with the powers of reproduction and sex. And because of their location in the back, the Kidneys were also associated with the spine, central nervous system, bone marrow and skeletal system as a whole. Healthy Kidney chi was thought to bestow longevity, strong teeth, lustrous hair and an active healthy sex life.

In modern scientific parlance, the *Jing* can be compared to our genetic inheritance – the various strengths and weaknesses that we derive from our parents at birth. It is also considered to be a finite substance – the kind of energy that, as you can perhaps imagine, is strong and vigorous in youth, but which ebbs away somewhat with the passing years. In chi kung, however, we believe we can help to preserve and strengthen this precious life force, to recharge the batteries, so to speak; to help slow down the ageing process and even reverse it for a while in some cases – back to a state of renewed vigour. So, I guess you could say there's hope for us all! (See Chapter 09 for a more in-depth discussion of the *Jing*.)

The Controller of Fluid

In the great medical classic, the *Nei Jing*, the Kidneys are described as 'The Controller of Fluid' – 'the official responsible for the creation of power', which, as we have seen, ties in very nicely with our knowledge of hormone secretion and with the adrenal glands. The *Nei Jing* also states in reference to the Kidneys that 'skill and ability stem from them'. This is interesting, because when the Kidney energy starts to wane with age we tend to become duller in a mental sense, even tending towards confusion and clumsiness. One of the most distressing symptoms of menopause (in men and women) is a certain decrease in vigour and co-ordination, with sometimes the bone density itself deteriorating. Providing we can look after our Kidneys, however – and we can do this by using exercises like chi kung – much of this deterioration can be averted or at least postponed, while *skill* is actually something that can and should increase with age, as with a good craftsman or master of any art. All this hinges on the health of the Kidney chi.

As you do this movement, therefore, try to visualize the strength of the energy of your kidney/adrenal complex, and of a warm glow of energy settled in the lumbar region and back. Dispel any feelings of anxiety or fear – the emotions most associated with the Water element when out of balance. Imagine a fine, blue light, a kind of fluorescent electrical blueness, emanating from the centre of your back and extending along either side of the spine and extending upwards also from the soles of your feet, cooling and calming the whole body but also giving you energy and strength at the same time.

Warming the kidneys

A useful adjunct to this exercise is to 'warm the kidneys'. The kidneys simply love to be kept warm. In traditional agricultural communities until very recently, workers exposed to cold winter winds during long hours of outdoor labour would often wrap the waist and kidney area in several layers of thick cloth, in addition to the normal outer layers of clothing – a sensible precaution born of long tradition and experience. So warm the kidneys now by bending forward slightly and placing your palms on the small of your back and gently rubbing up and down. You can do this before or after the chi kung exercise shown here – or *any time*, as part of your daily chi kung routine. It feels very pleasant, too. Just rub, gently for a few moments and think warm thoughts down into your palms and through into your lower back where the kidneys and adrenal glands are situated. The whole body will thank you for it.

Advanced practice

Returning to the chi kung, once you feel comfortable with the whole Ripples in the Stream sequence from this chapter, pay some attention to the following points.

The configuration of the hands can be varied during the circling movement. Try turning the palms up, as if holding a large ball or bowl in front of you as you go. The foot movements remain the same, of course. The fingers are still nicely separated, and the wrist is still curved in a relaxed manner – only with the palm facing upwards this time.

You can even include the palm up variation alongside the standard, palm down version, alternating during the same sequence from one to the other. Always keep the wrist relaxed, however. Many people do not realize that rotation of the hands is a movement that comes from the elbows, not the wrist. This turning of the wrist is accomplished from the movement of the ulna and radius bones at the elbow, which rotate, one against the other to turn the hand up or down. (This is why woodworkers can develop a painful elbow from overzealous use of the screwdriver.) So, however you wish to vary the aspect of the palms, do make sure the curved aspect between wrist and hand is not lost as the palms turn up or down.

Also, remember always that the circle your hands are making is a continuous movement, or that's how it should feel – not jerky in any sense. This is how the breath should be too in chi kung – continuous, smooth, without sudden inhalation or exhalation, without pause in between. Study the *Tai Chi T'u* symbol again (see page 19) and you will see again the perfect illustration of continuous movement and breath. Imagine how it would feel to travel around the *Tai Chi T'u* symbol, clockwise, changing from light to dark and back to light again, always moving. This is how the breath should feel, as well. This wonderful exercise shows us clearly how it can be matched to our physical movements.

There is a major acu-point situated on the sole of the foot called *yongquan* or 'the Bubbling Spring' (Figure 39). Try visualizing this as you go through your alternate rocking. See it being activated and imagine with each inhalation that you are drawing earth energy up from the ground towards the kidney area in the small of your back.

Finally, as you become more familiar and comfortable with all this, try to visualize the horizontal circle you are making with your hands as extending behind your body as well as in front of it. As you sit back on the rear foot allow your hands mentally to trace a half-circle behind your body, around the level of your kidneys and then forward once more, returning to the front

figure 39 *yongquan* – the Bubbling Spring

again. Make this imaginary circle as large as you like – ultimately you can make it the size of the horizon, another great circle, of course. There is actually a deep energy channel situated right here. This is the Dai Mai or Girdle Vessel – the only one in the body to flow in a horizontal plane rather than longitudinally. It runs all the way around the waist and exerts a special influence on the circulation of chi to the legs. It also flows from the Kidneys and connects to the genital area and reproductive organs. So you can also visualize energy circulating around the Girdle Vessel as you do this exercise! Always return to a state of inner focus, however, at the conclusion of your practice. Bring your attention back into the energy centre beneath your navel, the *tan tien* as it is called, and try to draw everything inwards to that one point of calm and stability before ending.

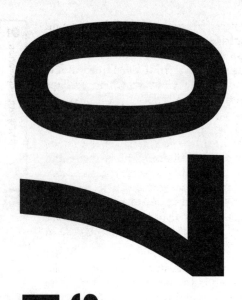

07

squeezing the ball

In this chapter you will learn:
- a relatively passive chi kung exercise with little movement
- about the earth element
- about the importance of proper nourishment.

With this exercise we complete the sequence of five around which our 'active' chi kung studies in this book revolve. It is one of the most universal and also one of the most simple of all chi kung exercises. Everyone can benefit from even just a few minutes of practising it. And, in my view, which is perhaps slightly biased, it is indispensable for anybody in the least bit involved with therapeutic body work such as massage, shiatsu, acupuncture and so on. This is because it very quickly puts us in touch with our own chi, which can be felt between the hands after just a few minutes, if not seconds of doing this exercise and therefore ultimately enables us to focus this energy more efficiently as we work. The more often you do it, in fact, the quicker you will be able to tap in to the sensation of chi between your hands. For the same reason, it is also the kind of exercise beloved by those engaged in the martial arts. Chi can be used in many different ways. It's up to the individual.

The sequence is laid out here in just two stages. So very simple. Almost everything here is focused in the wrists and elbows. The stance and the weight distribution remains the same throughout – centred 50/50 in both feet all the while.

Preparation

Perhaps nowhere has the breath been so instrumental in the shaping of the movements as in this exercise. You should be well-familiar by now with the concept of how the movements follow the breathing: that is, breathe first, then move, never the other way around. Here, what we have is simply *breathing in action*. The pattern itself is very simple, so once again, as with the last exercise, directions for the breathing are provided with the movements themselves.

Begin in the neutral standing position as outlined in Chapter 02 with your feet a little more than shoulder width apart and parallel to each other. Experienced practitioners can place the feet a little wider apart if they wish, but make sure the feet remain parallel and the knees well-bent.

Directions and breathing

1

Breathe in and raise the hands in front of you at about the height of your navel, palms facing each other. Imagine your hands are resting on opposite sides of a large ball or balloon (Figure 40).

figure 40 raise arms to hold ball

Tips

Try to sense the curve of the ball and mould your palms accordingly. Your fingers are relaxed, with none of the joints in any way locked straight. Just keep thinking of the spherical presence of that ball resting there between your palms and fingers, with the palm and all the fingers touching the surface.

Make sure your elbows are well-spaced from your sides and extended slightly forward from your body. Study the drawing carefully and keep returning to it to check your position.

Keep the shoulders relaxed and the muscles of the arms relaxed as well. The ball is not heavy. It is, literally, as light as air.

2

With the next natural exhalation, bring the hands just a little closer to each other and ... squeeze the ball! Imagine you are literally squeezing and applying pressure to the ball, which resists your squeeze a little, as if it is made of strong rubber or pumped up with air at a high pressure. Try to feel the resistance against your palms as you exhale.

figure 41 squeeze the ball

As you squeeze, the wrists and hands should alter shape from the previous position just outlined. Anatomically speaking the wrist joint is 'extended' now – so that there is an angle between your wrist and hand, the palms still facing each other, but with the fingers pointing forward (Figure 41).

Tips
The image used here of 'squeezing' is absolutely accurate in the sense that it tells us precisely how our hands should be placed. However, while keeping the 'squeezing' image firmly in mind, it is important not to apply any muscular tension whatsoever to the squeeze. To begin with, this may be difficult because while concentrating intently on the idea of *squeezing*, the muscles of the arm and wrist might, and usually do, tense up. Don't allow this to happen! Instead, just relax and let the arms 'float' – empty of tension. Think of this as a 'magic squeeze' – it just happens, without effort.

You can take as many breaths as you like while in position 2, until you start to feel the sensation of chi between your hands. Don't expect the sparks to fly – they won't. Just look out for a comfortable 'presence' or sensation there between your hands. Then, when you are ready to proceed, carry on as follows.

3

With the next natural inhalation, take away from your mind the intention of the squeeze and, relaxing your hands even more if possible, allow the pressure of the ball to push your hands apart. It really is as simple as that! Just allow the hands to return to the rounded, flexed position as described in step 1 and let the ball gently move your hands and forearms outwards again as you breathe in (Figure 42).

The cycle is now complete. You then simply repeat it, first squeezing the ball and then allowing it to push back against your hands. Keep repeating it, slowly, over and over, as many times as you like.

figure 42 open up again

Tips

The hands only separate and contract a short distance, of course. There are no large movements at all within this sequence. The size of the ball, therefore, the degree to which is contracts under your pressure with step 2 and subsequently presses your hands out again with 3, relies very much on individual preference. At first you might find that you have to draw the palms quite close together in order to feel the energy and feel the ball. But later on, the ball can become larger and it will still feel right.

As always, the breath here is significant. And because of the relative simplicity of this movement compared to those in previous chapters, we can really start to cultivate our abdominal breathing techniques here (see Chapter 02). The mind should also be entirely behind the breathing process. It is almost as if you are breathing pressure into the ball to initiate, later, the expansion of your palms. The breath moves the hands, therefore, not the muscles of the arms. Eventually, it will become apparent that the elbows are being controlled by the breathing also and that during the inhalation they tend to separate a little further from the sides of the body than during the squeeze – as if the ball is pushing against the forearms as well as the hands.

Keep repeating as many times as you wish.

What you can expect to feel

The feeling of energy between the hands can be quite remarkable, and even beginners often feel this pretty early on. Look out for a vibrational feeling or even of numbness or heat – anything that is sufficiently different to warrant attention – let it happen and let it increase. With extended practise you might feel some stiffness or tiredness in the wrists or forearms. Simply shake out or massage gently as described in Chapter 02 when dealing with energy blockages.

Sometimes, too, the hands may feel larger or you might notice they have become red, or have an almost swollen look to them as the blood circulation to the hands and fingers improves. In time, too, you might begin to really feel the presence of that ball – like a large, soft area of energy existing there between your arms! Generally, the whole abdominal area feels warm and energized.

More than any chi kung exercise, this one has the sensation of stability about it. Perhaps this is because of the particularly fixed and crouching stance. The feet do not move, the roots into the ground remain strong. We are therefore focusing on your relationship to the earth beneath us, with nature and the environment. It is an exercise which can quite literally put us back in touch with the natural world. With it, too, we can let go of some of our cares and worries. The world becomes a kinder, more supportive place and we feel more at peace inside as a result.

Mental focus – Squeezing the Ball and the Earth element

The emphasis on the abdominal area and the spherical surface of the ball accurately reflects the association of this movement with the Earth element of oriental culture and medicine. Earth is an unusual element, insofar as it is often associated with the end of each season rather than having a separate season all to itself. Having said this, however, the Chinese do have an additional fifth season called late summer, which is also represented by the Earth element.

When we think of this element, our thoughts naturally turn to ideas of stability, firmness, support and sustenance – all those qualities that the earth itself provides for us in abundance. Earth is at the centre of things. It is the great mothering principle of life, supporting and nurturing in character. This is why the final days of each season, when things settle down and there is little change in the climate, has such a strong resonance with this element.

Those organs within the body most associated with Earth are, not surprisingly, those that deal with digestion and sustenance: the stomach, pancreas and spleen. Although the spleen does not have much of a purpose in terms of digestion in Western physiology, in oriental medicine it is, like the pancreas with which it shares its anatomical location, seen as a vitally important adjunct to the function of the stomach. Almost all disorders of the digestive system, from the perspective of oriental medicine at any rate, have a corollary to an imbalance of Spleen energy.

The acu-channels associated with Earth – that is the Spleen and Stomach – run through the abdomen, along the front of the body and along the front aspect of the legs (Figure 6). Appropriately enough, they also tend to follow the pathway of the upper digestive tract, from the mouth, through the throat, oesophagus and stomach. In fact, the stomach acu-channel actually begins at the eyes. Among Eastern cultures it is often said that food should please the eye every bit as much as the taste buds. The preparation and presentation of food in Japan, for instance, can take on the dimensions of an art form, so that food, its anticipation and enjoyment can be a pleasure and a delight – a feature of gastronomy that is only rarely appreciated here in the West.

The Controller of Transportation and Transformation

As just mentioned, the Spleen in oriental medicine encompasses a far wider range of functions than those attributed to it in Western physiology.

According to the *Nei Jing* it is the official responsible for transportation and transformation of food essences throughout the body, while the Stomach takes the name of 'Controller of Rotting and Ripening'. All this makes sense when we consider the enormous and complex task the digestive system performs for us each and every day in first breaking down and then transforming basic raw material – food – into energy, nutrients, fluids, vitamins and minerals and all this in perfect proportion and in just the consistency that the body can assimilate in order to grow and maintain itself.

The first action that has to be performed in this process is the actual breakdown of food. The Chinese believe that the action of the Stomach begins at the mouth and that we should chew our food really thoroughly before swallowing. This enables it to be handled more efficiently by the 'rotting and ripening' function of the Stomach itself. The Spleen/pancreas combination can then transform and transport the energies of the digested food more easily. Failure of any one of these vital functions due to a disturbed digestive process can result in all manner of ailments, not only those connected with the stomach. Unless the nutrition can be transformed and transported to where it is needed, the cells of the body will simple starve. Symptoms can range from cold limbs and fatigue, to bowel disorders. At the very least we can develop obesity, along with all the dire implications that this all too common complaint has for us in terms of the health of the heart.

The Storehouse and Granaries

In its discussion of the Twelve Officials, the *Nei Jing* also informs us that the Stomach and Spleen are 'responsible for storehouses and granaries', or in other words for the supply of food and nutrition to the nation and so to the body. This reflects the enduring importance of these organs in the scheme of things – since to be responsible for the storehouses and granaries in a country plagued throughout its history by famine, was a position of immense responsibility in ancient China. 'Have you eaten today?' people still say to each other by way of greeting even in modern-day China. This relationship between a kind greeting and the process of nourishment is no accident, because proper digestion relies to a very large extent on emotional equilibrium – and vice versa.

Everyone knows how strongly the stomach can be affected by our emotions. From feeling butterflies when we are nervous, to feeling nauseous when we are upset, the stomach is like a mirror to our feelings. People who worry too much can develop ulcers in the stomach; and also those who devote too much time to purely cerebral activities and studies can often exhaust their Earth chi, leading to digestive problems and general weakness of the whole system. The word 'rumination', as well as being a term for digesting food, also means to think things over, of course – so there is even a connection established in our language between these two activities, the process of digestion and of thought. In fact, there are several popular phrases at large that refer to this relationship. We might, for example, find somebody's ideas 'hard to swallow', or 'unpalatable'. Can you think of any more?

With this exercise you are focusing on strengthening your digestive energies and getting in touch, too, with your attitudes to the whole process of taking in information. You are working on your experiences of what the words 'security', 'love', and 'support', really mean to you – your own internal *storehouses* and *granaries*.

See yourself in a position of strength, therefore – as if at the very centre of things – as you do this exercise. Tell yourself that you are in control of your life and of the circumstances in which you operate. Tell yourself that whatever comes your way can be dealt with calmly and efficiently – can be *digested*, in other words, and assimilated into your life without difficulty or risk. You are in charge, nourished by life and at one with the world about you.

Advanced practice

Once you feel comfortable with this exercise, pay some attention to the following points.

Be aware of the important *laogong* acu-point in the palms of the hands. This is an exit point of energy from the body – hence its importance for healing. *Laogong* can almost be seen, if you look at your palms and curl the fingers very slightly. There is a small depression usually visible in the centre, just beneath the palmists' headline below the base of the middle finger. If you cannot see it, you will almost certainly be able to feel its hollow with a very light touch (Figure 43).

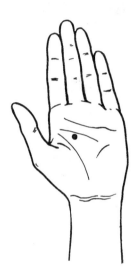

figure 43 *laogong* – Palace of Weariness

Laogong means Palace of Weariness – reflecting its clinical use as a point of tranquillity and calm when pressed or needled. It is as if such a potent point of energy can sometimes benefit from being pushed back, to calm it. And with this particular configuration of the hands, of course, the energy is not expended, but simply passes from one palm to the other. You may want to focus on this sensation if possible and try to build its intensity. It is almost as if you are generating energy internally as well as simply moving it around – putting it back inside. Any excess energy should therefore be sent down mentally to the body's natural energy storage centre, the *tan tien*, just beneath the navel. This 'sending down' of energy is best approached with the exhalation. For a more detailed discussion on the *tan tien* and on breathing generally, see Chapters 10 and 11.

As a variant on the regular squeezing movement, try raising the arms slightly on the in-breath, then lowering them with the out-breath, still squeezing the ball, of course. This is quiet difficult to achieve at first. So, to put it another way, the forearms come up and slightly outwards, with the expansion of the ball, then down and slightly inwards with the contraction, the squeezing of the ball. This produces an even stronger focus of energy in the lower abdomen – so well worth trying sometime.

08

embracing the tree – the art of stillness

In this chapter you will learn:
- a typical passive chi kung exercise using meditation
- the importance of stillness
- a deeper sense of awareness.

In the West we have a kind of fixation about how to keep fit and it usually consists of lots of running around, getting hot and bothered. Some people love it! If you are one of those people, that's fine. The exercise we are going to look at here, however, is all about stillness. That's right! Absolute stillness of body is what is called for here. Sure, the diaphragm or the abdominal muscles may contract a little with the breathing, or the shoulders might, if you are very lax about things, give the occasional nervous twitch. But by and large there is no movement – apart, that is, from the circulation of chi which, to a certain extent, will always be happening anyway.

Emmm! Sounds easy? You just try it!

First of all we ought to be clear about what we mean by being still. What is stillness, anyway? To some, it is going to bed and falling asleep. But how many people are really still when they sleep. Even here we all tend to turn and twist; we snore and grunt and whistle and scratch. Some people are so tense in their sleep they even grind their teeth!

Others might suggest that 'being still' is sitting in front of the TV. But is that really being still – when your mind is so occupied, tickled and pushed and manipulated this way and that? You laugh, you cry, fists clench, brows furrow – and jaws are often pretty active, too, as many of us like to nibble while we watch our favourite programmes. So what about other ways of being still? How about waiting for the bus? Anyone familiar with the British public transport system will realize straight away that this could be a pretty drawn-out affair. But do you really think that people are still while they are waiting for the bus? They shuffle their feet, look at their watch at least once every ten seconds. They natter, they shiver in the cold or fan themselves in the heat. No, we will not find examples of stillness here.

In fact, it is pretty safe to say, upon analysis, that we are never really, truly ever still. The moment we are compelled to be still or try to do it, we start to lose our composure completely. Do you remember what it was like in school, having to stand in the corner as a punishment for some misdemeanour? Wasn't easy, was it? So the kind of chi kung we are going to look at here, passive chi kung, in which there is no movement at all is, as you can probably imagine, both physically and emotionally extremely challenging. It is, in one sense at least, the most difficult thing we can ever attempt to do with our bodies. Forget all about climbing that mountain or running the marathon. We are talking *tough* here. At this level, chi kung is definitely not for wimps!

Standing like a Tree

The posture we are going to look at here is a universal exercise that is central to our understanding of not only chi kung but also much of oriental philosophy, medical theory and even some venerable and arcane studies such as Chinese alchemy. What you are about to learn here has connections to some of the most interesting and potentially rewarding pursuits ever undertaken by humankind. And this time I am not joking. To do this well is a lifetime pursuit. To comprehend it is an ambition worthy of anybody's time and study. And here is the nitty gritty – *time.* Passive chi kung – sometimes called *zhan zhuang* or 'Standing like a Tree' – requires monumental patience and dedication, not to mention a fair helping of self-discipline and, ultimately, trust.

In the East, even in these liberated times, if a teacher of chi kung or any similar subject asks a student to stand still for 10 to 20 minutes in one posture, he or she will do it. No questions asked. But here in the West it's different. How many people do you know who would be willing to do such a thing – and to do it every day, moreover, in the vicinity of family, children, dogs, pets, neighbours looking over the garden fence and so on?

Added to this, there is a matter of pride. Most of us do not take kindly to being ordered to do things that are uncomfortable, especially when the benefits seem ambiguous. Like it or not, this lack of clarification or proper explanation is a legendary feature of the Eastern arts such as chi kung, tai chi, yoga and so on. And, as anyone will know who has attended classes or workshops by prominent teachers of the subject, chi kung masters are invariably sparing with their words – masters of brevity, therefore, and with good reason! Think about it for a moment and put yourselves in their shoes. They may once upon a time have been very forthcoming – but after the one thousandth would-be student has asked the same questions, full of bright-eyed eagerness and enthusiasm for the moment, only to give up half an hour later when they became bored and to vanish from sight, the master soon runs out of enthusiasm for lengthy explanations.

Perhaps we need to be more patient here in the West, more trusting. I once heard a wonderful story about the great tai chi master, Cheng Man Ch'ing, who, shortly after arriving in the

United States and putting on a class to teach people the benefits of tai chi, set his group up in something like the chi kung posture you are about to learn here, then turned to walk away, only to find that everyone had immediately dropped their arms and were following him across the room to find out what came next! 'No, no!,' he said, 'I want you to *stay* like that.' It is not recorded how long the students did stay the way he wanted them to; but those who did would undoubtedly have been the wisest of the bunch.

So yes, there are certain practicalities to be overcome first, and certain internal obstacles, as well. But you can approach this phase of your study now with confidence, having learned the more active exercises earlier in this book and in particular the last one in Chapter 07 – Squeezing the Ball – which was excellent preparation for what comes next. With Squeezing the Ball, there was only minimal movement, remember – shaped around the breathing pattern. In fact, you may well have realized by now that the breathing is often more important than what the body is doing. If you have realized that, well done – top marks! The body has to be taken care of, of course, and the correct posture has to be cultivated, but once that is achieved the rest happens very much at an internal level. It is the next stage of refinement, if you like: letting go, more and more, of the familiar and, in the empty space that appears, allowing something new to enter.

Preparation

Taking into account all those points outlined in Chapter 02 about posture, begin now by standing upright with the feet parallel and a little more than shoulder-width apart. More experienced students can place the feet a little wider if they wish. Meanwhile, here is a quick reminder of the main points for posture – as important here as ever, if not more so:

1 Knees bent.
2 Spine upright.
3 Shoulders relaxed.
4 Feet not too close together.
5 Chest open.
6 Elbows rounded.
7 Find root.
8 Breathe through nose.
9 Use diaphragm.

Directions

1

Raise your hands to about chest height, palms facing inwards and with the elbows well-spaced out from your sides (Figure 44). The whole aspect of your arms is like somebody embracing a tree – rounded, therefore, with no sharp angles at the elbows or wrists. Even the fingers should partake of this curvaceous quality, so that if you were to extend the curved lines made by your arms and fingers, the lines would meet in the middle, completing a great half-circle in front of your chest.

figure 44 main pose, front view

Tips

The elbows should be lower than the hands and also ahead of the body line (Figure 45). Sometimes instructors will place a long stick or pole between the chest and the elbows of their students to make sure that these are in front of the body, not at the sides. This ensures a rounded scapula (shoulder blades) at the back which, in turn, helps promote energy circulation down from the spine and into the arms.

Another helpful picture to have in your mind while standing in this position is of a great ball or balloon that you are holding to your chest, the arms embracing the balloon.

Remember to keep the knees bent always – sink down! And always pay attention to your posture, making sure the legs have a rounded, arch-like appearance, like sitting on a horse. Some people also like to think of themselves being supported or sitting upon the surface of a large balloon as well. So the rounded, arch-like aspect of the legs would be wrapped around this balloon. This last image is OK, but don't lose touch with your root – that is, the feet should still feel well-planted into the ground.

figure 45 side view

2

Breathe into the abdomen and the major energy centre located just beneath the navel and a little way inwards, the *tan tien*. As we have seen earlier, in Chapter 02, this makes space for the diaphragm to descend and so allows the air to enter the lungs more easily. Breathe naturally, however. Don't force anything. As always, stick to your own natural rhythm and inclinations.

Tips

Sources differ on the precise location of the *tan tien*. Some say one and a half inches beneath the navel, others say three inches – all this depends on the size of the individual, however. Think of it as being a large area, rather than a small point, and eventually you will become aware of its location, which may vary slightly anyway, person to person. It is also located some distance inwards towards the spine – so not on the surface. Think inwardly!

By 'breathing' into the *tan tien*, we are speaking metaphorically, of course – directing the thoughts there, rather than the actual physical breath. Physiologically speaking, the breath must always go to the lungs which are higher up in the chest. This is inevitable. You would be in terrible trouble if the breath actually went into your stomach or abdomen! What we are talking about here is the essence of the breath – the chi. Send this down. Allow the tummy to expand a little with the in-breath as outlined on page 39. The abdomen will be responding to the inhalation anyway if you are using the diaphragm, but you should be focusing mentally on that area too, as if the air is being directed into the abdomen as well as the lungs.

3

Breathe out and allow the abdominal wall to sink back inwards again. As you do this, imagine the energy building up, condensing, stronger and stronger each time in the area of the *tan tien*. Alternatively, after several breaths, you can allow the energy to spread out on the exhalation, all through your body, filling it with light. See the light spreading out, a subtle radiance warming and invigorating every part of your body.

Tips

Keep your shoulders relaxed through all of this. Remember the action of the breathing takes place in the abdomen, facilitating the movement down and then up again of the diaphragm with each cycle, in-breath and out-breath.

That's it! That is all there is to this exercise – at least at this early stage. All you need to do now is to keep doing it. And keep doing it. *And keep doing it!* This is the hard bit. What usually happens is that you glance at your watch when you begin your practice session and it says, say, 8 o'clock. You look at it five minutes later and discover that, unfortunately it is still only 8.01! Time passes very slowly. One minute is unbelievably long.

Two minutes is an eternity. 'Why am I doing this?' you ask yourself. 'Is this some kind of joke? I can't feel any benefit from any of it at all. It's a waste of time, and my life is ticking away inexorably.' Don't worry. Everybody who has ever done passive, standing chi kung like this has felt the same way at one time or another – and probably continues to do so, now and again, if they care to admit it. But the benefits will come. Patience please!

How long?

To begin with you should try to sustain this position for no more than a couple of minutes. That is quite long enough in terms of physical exertion alone, especially if you don't cheat by unbending the knees when they start to ache. Later on you can increase this period if you wish. Those people who make passive chi kung part of their daily routine usually build up to 15 or 20 minutes. This is incredibly difficult and requires enormous dedication and self-discipline. You should not lose heart if you feel, probably with good reason, that this is not something you can ever manage yourself. Don't give up on it just because of that. Your estimation of your own capabilities can always change. Just do it! Even a couple of minutes of this wonderful exercise is better than nothing at all. And if combined with the more active chi kung movements shown earlier in this book, is extremely valuable and rewarding. Personally, I find it an ideal concluding phase to any session of active chi kung or tai chi – and a couple of minutes is sufficient in that context. It settles the mind and channels the energy perfectly back down into the *tan tien*.

What you can expect to feel

It has to be said that this unusually static position will likely lead to any number of minor nagging aches or pains. Even if you succeed in overcoming the mental impatience, the body will protest with feelings of stiffness and tension. Apart from the obvious discomfort in the arms and legs, you will discover that sites of old injuries, areas of scar tissue or muscular atrophy will all be highlighted as the chi attempts to assert itself and to move through the damaged or congested tissue. You might feel a shaking sensation or trembling also, or feelings of heat or cold in certain places. Try to stick with it, this is the energy at work.

People also sometimes experience a feeling of lopsidedness – as if one half of the body or one limb is in some sense different from the other. This, again, indicates imbalances of energy. For all these events, you should simply shake out or gently massage according to the suggestions outlined in Chapter 02 on dealing with energy blockages and then return to the exercise, trying to monitor whether you are, indeed, standing or holding yourself in an awkward or asymmetrical manner. Make sure the hips and shoulders are level and that one knee or elbow is not more bent than the other, that the head is not tilted to one side and so on.

Many of the sensations just described will take a while to overcome. We may well be talking in terms of weeks or even months here; another reason why patience is such an essential ingredient in this particular exercise.

On the positive side, you should begin to notice the chi building steadily in the *tan tien* area. People describe this sensation in different ways. For some it feels a little bit like the sensation of 'butterflies' in a nervous tummy. For others it is a trembling, a vibrational feeling that they get. It could be warmth, or even coolness. In other words, look out for *anything* – any sensation that is sufficiently different to warrant attention and then work on it, enhance it mentally until you can increase its presence.

Mental focus and advanced practice

The basic posture you have just learned and the little meditation about building the energy in the *tan tien* is really only a simple framework around which you can build the most interesting and advanced layers of experience. We will be looking at Taoist meditation in Chapters 10 and 11 that use postures of this kind, but for now, it is enough simply to focus on the sensation of warmth and energy that should be building in the *tan tien* and to try to enhance this with each breath, like a bellows fanning an ember. The bellows are, of course, your lungs.

Try to experience the sensation of a ball of energy between your hands, similar to the 'Squeezing the Ball' exercise in the previous chapter – only don't squeeze! Remember, no physical movement here. Just be aware of the energy field there in front of your body and any subtle pressure that this might be exerting. It is as if your energy field is somehow containing the energy of the ball, the one balancing the other in perfect equilibrium.

Try, also, to visualize the connectivity between the internal and the external – between the air within your body and the air outside. And allow that sensation to embrace the presence of a universal kind of chi, outside and within. See yourself as sharing in the experience of the outside world, of being part of it, at one with your environment and with all of nature. This is, of course, an experience of great depth and power. And that's just fine. Because with this, you are opening a window that will take you beyond simple physical exercise into a different and more enduring space. This opening, and what lies beyond, is an immensely exciting prospect and is what we will be devoting ourselves to in the remaining chapters of this book. Read on please – and explore! But above all keep on practising. Practice is everything, and without it, the window will simply close again.

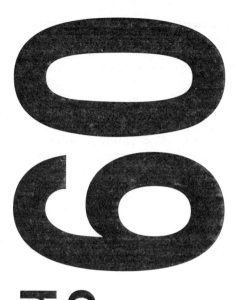

09

chi kung and health

In this chapter you will learn:
- more about health and the production of chi
- more about the causes of disease
- how to stimulate and clear the energy pathways.

It is strange, and rather ironic, that those government departments established to deal with health in our great nations are almost exclusively occupied with matters of *ill-health* instead. When was the last time you heard questions raised in the Commons or on the floor of Congress about how to keep people healthy? All the political arguments centre around illness, how to deal with it, how much money to spend on it and so on. Never about how to actually promote health. In fact, as we all know, ill-health is big business. The world's best-selling pharmaceutical drug, the multi-billion dollar Losec is designed to ease the symptoms of indigestion and stomach ulcers, while close on its heels comes Prozac, the world's most famous anti-depressant, with sales of $2.5 billion per annum in revenue for its makers. And although it might not be great news to the shareholders of the companies that hold the patents to these drugs, these illnesses are largely avoidable. Diet plays a significant part, of course. Stagnation of energy due to poor posture or lack of physical exercise can also become a serious problem, aggravated by the typical Western sedentary lifestyle. But above all, emotional imbalances due to worry, stress and poorly circulating chi within the body can be traced to the root of most digestive disorders *and* depression.

It should come as no surprises, therefore, that numerous studies have clearly demonstrated that regular and moderate exercise is easily the best preventive therapy for most common health problems. Exercise keeps the energies active and engaged; exercise keeps the mind occupied and less prone to worry. And among all the forms of exercise, those that make use of rhythmic movement combined with calm regular breathing – such as chi kung, yoga or tai chi – are by far the best in this respect. If people followed these precepts, think of all the money we could save on those drugs. And heaven knows what would happen to the pharmaceutical companies and the stock markets of the world if everybody suddenly decided to take up chi kung!

In this chapter we are going to take a more in-depth look at the health benefits of regular chi kung practice and to delve a little further into the fascinating world of oriental medicine – of which chi kung is considered to be a branch, of course. One of the best ways of approaching any aspect of this subject is by using the framework of the five elements: Wood, Fire, Earth, Metal and Water – all of which have, as we have seen, their own distinct energetic styles. But first of all, what about chi itself? We have already established that a good level of natural vitality helps to strengthen the immune system and helps to create an internal space in which illness finds it difficult to thrive or gain a foothold. But chi is more than just that. Chi, in fact, lies at the very foundation of all our physiological processes, paramount for the maintenance of life itself. Where does this vitality come from? And how do we convert it, store it and transport it around our bodies? These are important questions if we are to take our chi kung studies beyond the purely physical realm of repetitive movement and towards something more rewarding.

The production of chi

According to the classics of oriental medicine, the body's chi is derived from three main sources:

- *Jing* (inherited essence)
- food
- air.

Let's look at each of these before we see how they combine in practice.

Jing

We have already encountered the *Jing* in Chapter 06. It can, in part at least, be thought of in modern terms as our genetic make-up; the strengths or weaknesses that we inherit from our parents. Long ago, the Chinese recognized this process and they called it the 'inherited essence' of the individual: the *Jing*. And, just like our genetic make-up, this can vary greatly from person to person. It can be an enviable quality to have natural in-born strength, and we have all met people who, despite all manner of self-inflicted abuse, smoking, drinking, lack of exercise and so on, are somehow still blessed with astonishing levels of vitality. How do they do it? They have been born with an innately strong constitution – good *Jing*!

But it's not all just down to chance, to the cards we are dealt with at birth. Although the *Jing* tends to diminish with the passing of the years, it is still a substance over which we have a measure of control. Oriental medicine maintains that overwork or too much physical exercise when too young are ways in which *Jing* can be weakened. Men also lose much of their *Jing* through ejaculation, while women lose a fair proportion through childbirth and menstruation. Just like being given a great lump sum of cash at birth, we just keep spending it over the years until it is all gone. Some people are more prudent with this finite source of energy, others not so careful.

Incidentally, current scientific research into cell division in the body reveals some very interesting parallels. Situated at the end of the vital chromosomes which support the very basic building blocks of human life are to be found special fibres of DNA called telomeres. These microscopic fibres become smaller, actually shorten, with each repeated cell replication and are believed to signal ageing and death in the cells and eventually therefore in the whole human body. Normally, human cells divide about 75 times over a lifetime and it is this division and subsequent shortening and erosion of the telomeres at the end of the chromosomes that is implicated in the ageing process, like a kind of biological alarm clock, ticking away beneath the surface. Eventually the telomeres become too short to protect the chromosome. As they wear out, so do we – in other words, we could say the *Jing* becomes depleted.

How to look after your *Jing*
Another way of looking at it is to compare the *Jing* to an internal battery. It is obvious that if you punish any battery, say, for instance, your car battery by leaving the lights on all night, it soon runs down and has to be recharged, a process which is costly and can only be done a finite number of times, anyway. In the same sense, we can punish our *Jing* through excess – burning the proverbial candle at both ends. Hard work, vigorous exercise and sex are all fine in moderation – but there are natural limits. And therein lies the key: knowing these limits and not comparing our performance in any field with that of others. We all have different levels of tolerance, beyond which the poor old batteries simply run down.

The good news regarding the *Jing* is that we can preserve what we have by a reasonably moderate lifestyle and through exercise systems such as chi kung which actually strengthen the system rather than exhaust it. Combined with good wholesome food and clean air, a lot of damage can be avoided and even reversed to a certain extent. So, if you have led a life of utter excess up to now, don't despair. You probably enjoyed it – and that's great. Now, however, it's time to recharge the batteries. And not a moment too soon, I hear you say! Oh yes, of course, then there is that little matter of sex.

Here is a handy table based on information supplied in some of the old medical texts from the Sui Dynasty (sixth century) on the frequencies recommended for a man to ejaculate according to his age and state of health.

Age	Frequency	
	(good health)	(average health)
20	Twice a day	Once a day
30	Once a day	Every other day
40	Every 3 days	Every 4 days
50	Every 5 days	Every 10 days
60	Every 10 days	Every 20 days
70	Every 30 days	Not at all

table 1 frequency of ejaculation guidelines

These figures, incidentally, refer to the maximum frequency, not the minimum. If you are in poor health, less is always best. This is because the body is already drawing heavily on its internal reserves of energy to restore its balance and make itself well. Too much sex can inhibit this healing process and can even reverse it. Much of this is common sense anyway – though it is always surprising how many people push themselves beyond the limits of common sense when it comes to sex. This is unfortunate, because a good many cases of male impotence may be cured if only a little moderation could be bought to bear.

The classic texts tell us that we should also be a little more sparing during the cold seasons of autumn and winter, when we need more energy for warming and sustaining the internal processes. From 70 years of age onwards, moreover, it was clearly considered wise to conserve the seed with great care.

I once delivered a lecture that included this subject to a group of health practitioners. At the conclusion, the secretary of the group thanked me and said he had been especially interested in the frequency of sexual activity suggested by my presentation and would speak with his wife on this very subject that coming evening. He declined, however, to make it clear whether he would be urging an adjustment towards a higher or a lower figure.

Actually, it is important here to keep a sense of proportion and to bear in mind that the table does not imply that all forms of sexual activity should be restricted, because, (and this may come as a surprise to many a Western male), sex does not necessarily have to conclude with ejaculation! Advanced sexual practices as exemplified by the Taoist and Tantric traditions of the East outline numerous techniques and methods of increasing sexual performance and pleasure and these advocate considerable moderation in this respect. It also enables those engaged in these practises to channel and enhance their own internal energies. All this is, unfortunately, beyond the scope of this book – but is well worth a little exploration.

Chi from food

Chi also comes from external sources, namely from food and from the air, both of which need to be of good quality if chi production is to be strong. Let's look at food first. The type of chi we derive from food is called *gu chi* – the result of the digestion process.

Computer programmers have a saying: 'Rubbish in, rubbish out.' In other words if your programming is poor, the workings of the program will be poor, too, and any errors magnified. The same goes for the food that we eat. Quality is paramount. But what is quality? And what is good food? Much has been written, many arguments have raged and many reputations have been built and destroyed over food and rarely do we find the fickle hand of fashion at work so pervasively as in the world of diet. At one time it is virtually suicidal to allow the slightest morsel of butter to enter our mouths, the next day we learn that its 'healthy' substitute, margarine, is full of dastardly chemicals that can cause illness. At one time we should all be dieting on cold salads and fruit juice to preserve our very soul, at another time it's all down to the virtues of potatoes and beans! Actually, we can all be forgiven for being a little confused.

Real food

According to the time-honoured principles of oriental medicine, however, we find a consistency of ideas and advice on diet which has not changed much over the centuries. Generally, we are advised to eat wholesome foods that are in some sense 'live' – that is, ones that are not processed or preserved for long periods. Food should generally be cooked, moreover, in order that the body can extract the vitality and essence. Perhaps more obviously, it should not contain toxins or poisons. Unfortunately, most modern processed foods (including many of those found in the Far East) are not only denatured and void of natural chi, but also contain numerous chemicals and additives which ultimately result in a toxic build-up within the body.

Our digestive systems are sensitive beasts and they can best cope with foods that are still in their natural state, fresh vegetables and grains, combined with some dairy produce and meat in moderation. These foods provide all of the vitamins and minerals, protein and carbohydrates we could ever possibly need. Fruit is of less importance than might be imagined in this scheme of things and during the winter months, and particularly in the more northern, temperate climates, is thought to be counterproductive if taken in excess. This is due to its strong cooling effect, which can weaken the digestive energies. The very best rule of thumb is usually to eat what is in season and to eat what grows or can be reared in your own climate and locality. Cook it nicely and eat it fresh, without preserving with chemicals. Also, in our own very difficult times of intensive crop spraying and factory-reared livestock it is best to eat foods that are certified organic as often as possible.

In this way, a well-fed, warmed and regularly nourished digestive system is far better placed for the vital task of transformation and transportation of food essences around the body than one which is starved and malnourished. This is why severe crash diets, or those diets based on cold raw foods, often leave the recipient in a worse state than at the start. They have starved their digestive energies and weakened them, often irreparably.

A matter of taste

The classic text, the *Su Wen*, says of the Stomach and Spleen that 'the five tastes stem from them'. The Chinese understand taste in terms of five distinct flavours, that correspond to the five elements: sour, bitter, sweet, pungent and salt corresponding to Wood, Fire, Earth, Metal and Water respectively. Often we can diagnose imbalances in one or more of the elements by individual preferences or dislikes for these flavours. Someone who craves salty food incessantly might, therefore, have an imbalance of the Water element, and therefore a weakness of the Kidneys. Sweetness and the Spleen are also very relevant since the Spleen and pancreas are usually treated as synonymous in modern oriental medical theory. One of the most serious and increasingly present illnesses in our culture at present is sugar diabetes. This is a pancreatic illness and manifests extreme reactions to sugar intake – the sweet taste, in other words.

Table 2 contains a list of foods considered to have especially powerful associations with the five tastes.

Sour	Lemon, grapefruit, grape, apple, apricot, sour plums, blackberry, blackcurrant, gooseberry, olives, cheese, vinegar, trout and most green, leafy vegetables
Bitter	Lettuce, asparagus, broccoli, celery, chicory, radish, watercress, rocket, alfalfa, beer, dark chocolate, raspberry leaf tea
Sweet	Most foods containing sugar, sweets, cakes, dates, honey, carrot, cherry, chicken, cucumber, lamb, oats, peach, rice, spinach, tomato, walnut, milk, sweet wines, sherry
Pungent	Spicy foods, including cloves, cumin, marjoram, cayenne pepper, rosemary, mint, nutmeg, ginger, cinnamon, mustard, garlic, green pepper, cabbage, leek, wheat germ, dry wine, turnip
Salty	Salty foods and sea foods – crab, lobster, mussels, oyster, sardines, kelp (seaweed) – barley, duck, ham, pork

table 2 the five tastes and foods most closely associated with them

It is considered helpful if our diet can contain a balance of the five tastes as this creates variety and ensures good digestion. Sour foods, for instance, are astringent in their action on the body, while bitter foods are purging and cooling. Moderately sweet foods (not sugary sweet, which are generally poor foods anyway) can tonify the digestive system. Pungent foods, meanwhile, are valuable because they can help disperse and move obstructions in chi and blood flow, while salty tasting foods (not necessarily salt itself) can act to balance our body fluids so that we retain the right amount of moisture in our systems.

Chi from air

Our final source of chi comes from the air that we breathe. The Lungs are the receptors of this energy and the chi is, as we have seen, found at its strongest and most plentiful in clean, fresh air. So rural areas are obviously better than urban ones in this respect. If we are forced or choose to work and live in big cities, however, it is important to get some decent air every once in a while. Short breaks or walks in places where the air is clean are really essential. This is why people in big cities in China and the Far East tend to take to the parks and open spaces early in the morning to do their chi kung or other exercises – since the pollution has not yet become too serious at that time of the day. Smoke, dust, exhaust fumes, all these sap the air of its natural negative ionized particles (see page 12) and therefore of its vitality as well: *its chi*. It is a testimony to chi kung's great efficacy that it enables us to get our fair share of chi from even comparatively unwholesome air, but if you can practise somewhere pleasant, as well – outdoors, in a park or garden or by the sea – you will derive even greater benefits.

Inspiration and communication

The *Nei Jing* describes the Official of the Lungs as 'The Receiver of Chi from the Heavens'. In this sense, it is useful to bear in mind that 'the heavens' do not have a religious connotation; they are simply what is above and around us. But air does have an interesting effect on our inner state. Countless great artists and composers from all ages have drawn inspiration from country walks and the very word 'inspiration' is, of course, an alternative term for breathing in. We can become inspired from breathing, therefore, and from breathing well.

It may sound obvious, but we often forget the simple fact that air is the only thing outside us that we actually take in at every moment of the day, constantly. By the act of breathing, we become part of our environment, sharing continually in what is outside us. Consequently, we develop patterns of respiration according to our lifestyle and the circumstances in which we live and work. If the air is wholesome we are more likely to breathe more easily and confidently and the vital interchange of energies with our surrounds is achieved without strain. If, however, the air is a constant source of smells, dust and other unpleasant sensations, we can quickly develop a defensive attitude mentally and emotionally to our surroundings and to those things that come our way. We can become isolated, cut off and ill at ease. The effects of atmospheric pollution on the mind and the emotions are just as pernicious in many respects, therefore, as carbon monoxide and diesel fumes on the body.

The nervous system and breathing

When we breathe deeply and easily the body's parasympathetic nervous system is stimulated. The parasympathetic is part of our autonomic nervous system that helps the body to rest and to nourish and renew itself through the digestive process. It is the opposite to the sympathetic nervous system, which is mobilized during times of stress and tension – the fight or flight instincts left over from our primitive past, when we were more likely to be chased by a wild animal than be caught in a traffic jam – but the internal effects are the same. That's the sympathetic response: hyperactive, sometimes fearful, in which the breathing often becomes laboured and erratic. The breath is therefore like a switch between the sympathetic and the more tranquil parasympathetic. It is something we can control to a certain extent through our own efforts. Rather than allowing the emotions to control our breathing, therefore, we can reverse the equation and control our inner state through the way we breathe!

Tests measuring the electromagnetic resonance of the brain confirm that our brains shift into what is termed the 'alpha state' of relaxation and deep rest during chi kung breathing exercises, a state in which not only the digestion but the body's immune function, too, can work at its optimal level. This is why chi kung helps us feel more in tune with our emotions and thoughts. To take this a step further, we could even say that good breathing is a bridge between the conscious and unconscious minds. Through contact with our parasympathetic or alpha state, we can go deeper into our own inner self than might otherwise be the case. This in turn enables us to contact our creative energies, to solve problems and to comprehend and communicate our needs and feelings more effectively. What a difference we can make to our daily lives simply through good breathing!

The internal engine

So now we have the formula:

Jing + food + air = chi

Separately, they are of little value: we cannot live by food alone or air alone. All three have to converge together in the body to create the internal energy that sustains us. Again, we can think of this in mechanical terms if you like. Think of the way a car engine works. Our food can be compared to the fuel we put into our cars, which has to be mixed with air to be of use – since everything needs oxygen to make it burn. This occurs in the body, too – the air, in this case, coming via the lungs. But air and fuel are not enough. There has to be a source of energy to ignite this mixture – and this is the purpose of the spark plugs in the car engine. The *Jing* is like the spark plugs of the body, it makes everything fire up and work properly.

Chi kung exercise particularly strengthens the function of the Lungs, Stomach and Spleen – those organs most responsible for receiving and processing the external chi of food and air. All these ingredients are then thought to be combined in the chest area – a place called the 'Upper Sea of Chi'. The chi is processed here and once this potent mixture is refined and activated with the aid of the *Jing*, it spreads out all over the body. In this, it functions in two distinct ways: first, to protect and then to nourish – each of which is essential for our health and well-being.

The protective chi: the body's defensive shield

We saw in Chapter 05 how the vital energy can circulate in the form of a defensive shield, the *wei chi*, close to the surface of the body where it performs a very special task for each and every one of us. This kind of chi is related to the immune system of the body, protecting us from external pathogens. The Lungs play an important part in the storage and distribution of this particular form of vital energy and, indeed, whenever we succumb to illness it often takes the form of a respiratory disease first – i.e. sore throat, runny nose, coughs and sneezes etc. This is the body's defence system, the protective chi, trying to combat any invading pathogenic factor and destroy it.

These pathogenic factors, the 'external evils' as they were termed, were the nearest the ancient Chinese could penetrate to an understanding of bacteria and viruses. They did not possess our vast array of scientific instruments, microscopes and laboratories to explore these things. Instead, they saw disease, in part at least, as being connected with those climatic conditions that appeared to aggravate the illness in question. If cold made it worse – for example, some rheumatic conditions – then 'cold' was the term given to the illness. So the main external evils were Wind, Damp, Cold, Heat and Dryness. It is the main occupation of the protective chi to combat these. If the levels of *wei chi* in the body are strong, the invading pathogens will be fought off successfully – but if not, we are likely to go on to develop a more chronic illness.

Table 3 gives the kinds of symptoms belonging to each of the external pathogenic factors and which can easily arise if we are exposed to them in excess.

Cold	Fixed pains in joints, backache, urinary, kidney, bowel and other digestive problems, pre-menstrual pain, infertility
Wind	Respiratory diseases, headaches, stiff necks, hay fever, skin complaints and general muscular aches and pains that 'wander'
Summer heat	Sun-stroke, dehydration, dizziness, in extreme cases inflammatory illnesses, severe headaches, fever and mental disorientation
Damp	Oedema, swollen, aching joints and muscles, fungal infections, phlegmy conditions, overall feelings of congestion and malaise
Dryness	Dry cough, dry throat, sore eyes, flaky and dry skin, constipation

table 3 external pathogenic factors and their symptoms

These climatic factors are as relevant for us today as ever because they can hasten the onset of all manner of illness, either through damaging the body's immunity or by aggravating already existing internal weaknesses or viral infections. With a little care and a few common sense precautions, of course, we can easily take steps to avoid the worst consequences of these – by wrapping up in cold, windy weather, for instance, by protecting vulnerable areas such as the throat, head and kidneys; by avoiding excessively hot, dry or damp conditions; removing damp clothes and changing into dry ones whenever possible, and not venturing outside with damp hair on a cold day. In short, all the things that grandma used to urge us to do when we were children. She would also, at the same time, probably have made sure we avoided draughts and that our domestic environment was warm, dry and wholesome. Good old grandma! She was fortunate to have lived in an age that still preserved some common sense wisdom in regard to matters of health.

All this is important for us because chi kung helps to cultivate the *wei chi* and to strengthen the defensive shield. Those who practise regularly will not succumb so easily to many of the above symptoms and they will rarely suffer from colds or flu – a good sign, indicating that the immune system is in good shape, zapping all those nasty viruses and bacteria and working away to keep the body fit and well at all levels, inside and out.

Incidentally, the *wei chi* is also thought to have a powerful effect on the skin, the outermost defensive layer, moistening it and controlling the opening and closing of the pores – in other words perspiration – which, again, explains the rationale among those familiar with folk medicine and home remedies to promote sweating in order to rid the body of colds and flu.

Nourishing chi: the energy pathways

Apart from its sterling work in defending us from external pathogens, chi also works deep within the body to sustain the vital organs and life-support systems. The chi that works in this way is called the nourishing chi or *ying chi*. This is the chi that flows along the channels or meridians of the body, and at this stage it might be worth recapping somewhat on the structure of this system.

As you may recall, the acu-channels tend to take their name from the organs through which they pass and so therefore each channel/organ also belongs to one of the five elements. For instance, the Lung acu-channel that runs along the thumb side of the arm has an energetic correspondence to the Metal element, while at the same time passing through the organ of the Lung. Therefore, certain patterns of disharmony in our health can be associated with the quality of energy in these channels. Table 4 should help put all this in context. As you can see, with the exception of Fire, each element has one yin and one coupled yang organ associated with it.

Element	Yin organ/channel	Yang organ/channel
Wood	Liver	Gall Bladder
Fire	Heart Pericardium	Small Intestine Triple Burner
Earth	Spleen	Stomach
Metal	Lungs	Large intestine
Water	Kidneys	Bladder

table 4 the Five Elements and their corresponding yin and yang organs

A healthy system will send its own nourishing chi to all of these organs automatically. But as we saw briefly in Chapter 02, one of the ways in which people have traditionally moved energy around the channels and helped themselves to clear blockages or weaknesses is through gentle percussive techniques – that is patting or pressing very lightly with their palms or fingers along the length of these channels. This practice is a very useful therapeutic device and is often recommended to patients recovering from illness. It is always worth trying this yourself, especially if you feel there are parts of your body where stiffness or weakness seems to exist. Here are five simple routines, one for each element. They are suitable for most people, but should be avoided during pregnancy. Also, if you have brittle bones (osteoporosis) or any major areas of inflammation, proceed with caution and contact your doctor first.

Wood

Look again at Figure 2, on page 9.

Gently tap with the palms of your hands down the top of the shoulders and then along each side of the body in turn. When you come to the hip area, you can use both palms or loosely folded fists to pat down the outside of the legs gently, then over the top of the feet and gently up the inside of the legs. Do this several times, trying to establish a rhythm, like drumming. All these areas have a focus of central energy at the location of the Liver and Gall Bladder organs, which are situated just behind the lower ribcage on the right. Place your left palm there, and with your right palm resting gently on top of the back of the left hand, slowly brush the left palm inwards and slightly upwards towards the centre line of the body. Do this very lightly, please, and repeat several times – for as long as you wish until you have the sensation of any congestion that might be lurking there becoming dispersed. It feels good!

Fire

Check out Figure 3 again, on page 9.

With a loose, relaxed fist, gently pat along and down the inside of the arm and with special emphasis on the little finger side, pat upwards along the outside of the arm too. Massage into your palm with the opposite thumb, on the area right in the centre and the *laogong* acu-point (Figure 43). Then, with your fingers together, gently stroke from the chest towards the top of the arms. Fire energies tend to focus in the chest, so with your palms resting very lightly on this area, make a few small rotational movements of the hands to disperse any stagnant energy there. Try to bring the energy down from the centre. Take a good breath between these movements, too, and sigh if you wish because you may be dispersing a lot of emotional baggage at the same time.

Metal

Take another look at Figure 4, on page 10.

With a very loose and gentle fist, lightly tap all the way down the soft, inside edge of the thumb side of the arm, and then rotate the arm and tap up along the outer, yang aspect – the hairier side, that is (for some of us). Pay special attention to the muscles that originate at the elbow, which are often slightly tender. Then try out your Tarzan imitation with a very gentle rhythmic patting on the upper chest area. Just pat – either with palms or very soft fists. Try pressing lightly with your thumbs under the collar bones, too – from the centre outwards. All this helps to disperse stagnant energy from the Lungs.

Water

Refer back to Figure 5, on page 11, for this one.

With your hands on the back of your head, gentle probe with the thumbs beneath the ridge of the occiput, either side of the neck bones. Massage the back of the neck with your fingertips. Then, bending slightly forward and placing the hands on the lower back, gently tap along the sides of the spine. At the kidney area in the small of the back, use your palms to gently rub (see warming the kidneys in Chapter 06). Hold for a while, palms against the kidneys with stationary pressure, then bend forward again and proceed downwards with rhythmic tapping over the buttocks and down the back of the legs. Take special care if you have any prominent veins – these don't like being thumped. Continue working right down to the tip of the little toe and pinch it! You can then tap up the inside rear aspect of the legs if you wish.

Earth

Have another look at Figure 6, on page 11.

Gently pat down the front of the body, either side of the centre line (women should avoid the breasts) and down either side of the abdomen. Continue patting down the outer aspect of the front of the leg, across the bridge of the foot and then up the inside aspect of the front of the leg, back to the groin. The focus of these energies lies in the area of the Spleen, which is just behind the lower portion of the left ribcage. Place your right palm here and, with the left palm resting lightly on the back of your right hand, brush the palm inwards and slightly upwards towards the centre line. Do this several times until you feel satisfied that any stagnation of energy that might be situated there is dispersed. Don't do this on a full stomach, however.

The Chinese clock

One of the most interesting ways of looking at the functions of the channels and their respective organs comes from what is called the Chinese clock. This is not some special, fiendish method of time-keeping employed by the Chinese, but a way of looking at the performance of each of the organs in terms of the

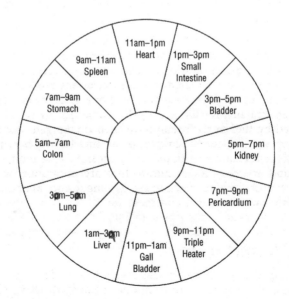

figure 46 Chinese clock

diurnal cycle – the time of day. Each organ and channel has a time of peak performance, a two-hour period when it receives more energy than any of the other organs. For example, the Heart is at its strongest around midday – convenient, since that is when most of us are at our most active, working or playing hard. Exactly 12 hours after its peak is always the least active time of any organ – so in the case of the Heart, midnight, the time when we sleep (usually). The nourishing chi, moreover, flows from one organ to the next according to the same principles of the Chinese clock. So after the ascendancy of the Heart, for example around midday, the energy passes to the Small Intestines, and from there to the Kidneys and so on. (See Figure 46 for a representation of the Chinese clock in action.)

Much of this makes sense when we review our daily activities. The Stomach is at its best at breakfast time, when it can digest and make use of quite substantial amounts of food. So the old adage of eating breakfast like a king, lunch like a prince but dinner like a pauper is based on sound reason. The Colon, by way of contrast, is active much earlier in the morning, so we can empty our bowels and get on with our day feeling fresh and cleansed. The liver, meanwhile, kicks in around the early hours, when our blood is still and the body at rest. Much of the blood goes to the Liver and is stored there at this time while we sleep. The main thrust of all these factors, however, is the idea of circulation – of chi passing unimpeded from one organ and channel to the next over the 24-hour period.

Chi kung helps boost this circulation of energy through the channels by removing blockages and encouraging the flow. Each channel has a point or area of the body where the chi exits and enters. These areas where exit and entry points are located tend to be either in the chest area and head or else at the extremities, the feet and hands. These are, of course, precisely the areas targeted by the exercises you have been doing from this book. So keep up the good work, and the internal clock will run smoothly; not too fast, not too slow, but simply running on time according to the laws of nature that are constantly working away for us, behind the scenes, helping us to maintain our optimal physical state at all times.

The grand tour

To put all this into context, let's take a tour of the body, based on the daily passage of chi from one organ to the next. On the way, we will have the opportunity of exploring the functions of the elements once more, the organs to which they belong and of those illnesses experienced when these are out of balance.

The tour begins with the Metal element and the Lungs. The Lungs are at their strongest very early in the morning and this is why chi kung and tai chi are most beneficial for us at this time. This is not to say that you should leap out of bed at 3.00 a.m. and begin your exercises! The Lung energy is at its peak then, that's all. It is still pretty strong at, say, 7.00 a.m. or 8.00 a.m. – so don't worry.

After the Lungs, the largest proportion of chi is sent to the Colon. This is the best time to empty the bowels, therefore – the easiest time, in fact, if we can get into the habit. As we saw in Chapter 05, letting go regularly in this way helps us to free off mentally as well. It is amazing how many people are mentally constipated simply because they do not look after their bowels.

Once the bowels are emptied we can comfortably settle down to the first meal of the day, breakfast. This is the time when our element of nourishment kicks in – the Earth element, running at its peak from 7.00 a.m. to 11.00 a.m., beginning with the Stomach. This is followed by the Spleen/pancreas to aid digestion, transformation and transportation of food essences. So, without doubt, this is the best time of the day to metabolize our food quickly and efficiently. How odd that people turn this clever idea completely on its head and usually eat late in the evening instead, the very time when the digestive energies are at their *lowest*. People invite one another out to dinner as a mark of their friendship or love. If we really loved somebody, we should actually invite them over for breakfast! 'Darling,' we would say, 'how about breakfast tomorrow morning?' Might raise a few eyebrows.

The Fire element takes over from 11.00 a.m. and carries on until 3.00 p.m. This time of the day is all about circulation – of circulating blood and oxygen to give us energy for work and play and of absorbing and circulating food within the blood stream, absorbed by the Small Intestine, of course. This is a period of great capability, when we can work hard in a physical sense, team up with others and exchange ideas and really get things done. Fire, remember, is a very creative and social element.

From around 3.00 p.m. to 7.00 p.m. it is the turn of the Water element to kick in – the Bladder first, then the Kidneys. These organs helps to regulate our internal fluid balances and maintain the correct blood pressure. They also cleanse the body of impurities, while the adrenal glands situated on top of the kidneys provide us with impetus and power to keep going through the afternoon. People often need a nap at this time of the day, particularly the elderly, because their Kidneys are running out of steam. A short catnap or siesta at this time of the day is often very beneficial, even for those in optimal health. In the winter months this is especially helpful in conserving our energies.

After 7.00 p.m. the Triple Burner and Pericardium take over. These are unusual energies in so far as one, the Triple Burner, has no organ belonging to it at all, while the other, the Pericardium, is the name given to the protective layer of tissue around the heart. Together they help to circulate chi and regulate body fluids, to harmonize our emotions and help us socialize, come together or unwind at the end of the day.

From 11.00 p.m. onwards, the Wood element makes its presence felt. Wood is regulated by the Liver. This is when the Blood settles down and is stored in the Liver. It is a time of rest and sleep, allowing the Liver and the hundreds of different regulatory functions it performs for us, often simultaneously, to get on with its task. Some people are hyperactive at this time. They either cannot get to sleep or else they wake in the night. This can be a sign of a disturbed Wood element – although there are many other possible causes.

After this, the Lungs come into play once more and the whole cycle begins over again. Watch and monitor your body closely for a while and see where your 'best time' of the day lies. What time is your worst? When do you feel at your weakest or most restless? These times can tell you a lot about your internal chemistry. The good news is that with regular chi kung practice the internal clock becomes more regulated and balanced and you can begin to organize your life according to the laws of nature. This takes a certain degree of mental focus, of course – to have the strength to make changes if they need to be made. And it is to this area and the cultivation of the necessary mental faculties that we will turn to next.

chi kung and meditation

In this chapter you will learn:
- more about thought and meditation
- about Li and K'an – fire and water
- how to disperse areas of emotional disharmony.

For not nature only, but man's being has its seasons, its sequence of Spring and Autumn, Summer and Winter.

Chuang T'zu

Chi kung is not just about breathing or the circulation of energy through the channels. It is also very much about getting the mind and the emotions sorted. Negative emotions, in particular, are critical to the state of our health since they draw extensively upon our internal energies and can quickly sap the strength from our vital organs. Unpleasant feelings, agitation, anger, grief and worry, can all contribute to the onset of disease. It works both ways, moreover. Emotional negativity can also be an outcome of already existing internal disharmony within the organs and channels.

The Chinese understood the power of emotions long ago and the classics of medicine written during those times make it very clear the extent to which these connections exist between the body and mind and how easily one can affect the other. In the West, unfortunately, we are only just able to hang on to the idea of any form of mental or spiritual energy existing at all, let alone thinking of each organ of the body having its own separate version! And that our emotions could be even indirectly responsible for disease is a concept only grudgingly ac-knowledged at present by the phrase 'psychosomatic illness' – a very limiting and unsatisfactory blanket term, as if the illnesses in question are in some sense unreal, 'all in the mind'. This comes nowhere close to the detailed understanding of the correspondences developed by the acupuncturists and herbalists of ancient China.

The connections discovered all those centuries ago are still very much relevant today, of course, and are widely used in modern clinical practice for both diagnosing and curing numerous complaints, including sometimes those of a chronic and seemingly intractable nature. So, for example, you sometimes find that people who are continuously angry may also suffer from gallstones or a diseased Liver, while those who are constantly laughing and over-effusive have a problem with the Heart. Sometimes a lack of an emotion can be just as damaging as an excess of one. It indicates that energy is being repressed somewhere. Needing to be overassertive and domineering, for instance, can certainly be linked to an imbalance of the Liver – but behaving in the opposite way, being indecisive and weak-willed (lily-livered), can also originate from the same source. An absence of the faculty to experience joy is every bit as damaging to the Heart as being hooked on the endless treadmill of noise and commotion often referred to as 'having fun'. In other words, any extreme of emotion, excessive or deficient, indicates an imbalance that can upset our internal energies and unless we take this into account, it does not matter how diligently we practise the physical side of our chi kung, the results will be disappointing. Power is useless without control. And self-control can only arise when the emotions are balanced.

Cycles of energy

As ever, the best way to approach this aspect of chi kung is via the Five Elements. The Taoist philosophers of ancient China and the medical practitioners of those times (often they were one and the same) saw the elements not as static entities, but as phases of energy which would change one into the other and support and influence each other as well. This has come to be represented in diagrammatic form (Figure 47).

On this diagram there are two cycles represented, traditionally known as a generative (*sheng*) cycle and a controlling (*ke*) cycle. The generative cycle corresponds to the progress of the five seasons of Chinese culture: spring (Wood), summer (Fire), late

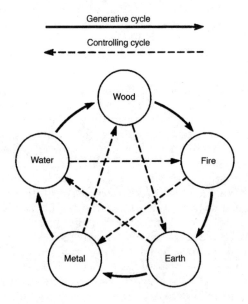

figure 47 five elements star

summer (Earth), autumn (Metal) and winter (Water). It is easy
to see how the ancient, agricultural communities of China
perceived this cycle in the world around them. The internal five-
pointed star, meanwhile, traces out a more controlling, in some
sense destructive sequence. So Wood controls Earth (growing
trees binds the earth with roots); Earth controls Water (by
absorbing it and channelling it); Water controls Fire (dowses the
flames); Fire controls Metal (fire melts metal); and finally Metal
controls Wood (cuts it and shapes it).

Taken all together, the elements must inevitably influence each
other according to these cycles. A deficiency in one can lead to
weakness in another; and the same with excess – with too much
of one overacting on another. Here, then, are the major
emotions according to their elements, the organs that pertain to
them and the consequences to other elements if these are out of
balance (refer also to Figure 48).

Wood, anger and frustration

Anger frequently comes directly from the Liver. It is also an
emotion that can damage that organ and its associated organ
the Gall Bladder. Along with frustration or feelings of
oppression, it inhibits the smooth flow of chi throughout the

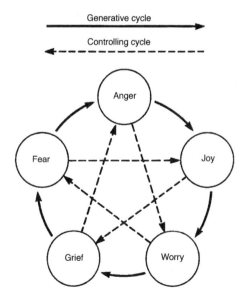

figure 48 five emotions star

body, leading to a general stagnation of energy and blood circulation, stiff joints and muscles, abdominal, shoulder and neck pain, migraines, irritable bowel syndrome and pre-menstrual tension.

Wood nourishes Fire in the *sheng* cycle and without a healthy, creative Wood phase to our energies we would be unable to grow and mature to our full potential. The springtime of youth becomes a poor and miserable summer, therefore. Wood also controls Earth in the *ke* cycle and an excess of Wood energy can take away our sense of stability and calm. Hyperactivity, restlessness and abandoned plans can result, 'getting nowhere fast'.

Fire and joy

What is meant by 'joy' here is overexuberance, manic behaviour, a restless drive for overstimulation which exhausts the Heart energies of the body. Insomnia, palpitations and hypertension can result over time. Shock is considered to have similar consequences, with its well-documented effects on the Heart – although shock can also affect the Kidneys.

In the *sheng* cycle, Fire nourishes Earth. When our natural exuberance and joyfulness are directed constructively, in building relationships and providing inspiration to ourselves and others, the results are enduring and real. Summer brings forth its harvest in late summer, the time of Earth. Children and families grow to maturity. While in the *ke* cycle, Fire controls Metal, helping to disperse grief and sorrow with laughter and pleasure. Laughter is considered by some to be an excellent therapy, the perfect antidote to sadness and grieving.

Earth, worry and overthinking

These feelings affect the Stomach and digestive system generally. We all know people who have indigestion or ulcers from worry or overthinking. But also lethargy, cold limbs, poor appetite, prolapse of organs, loose bowels, heavy periods and vascular weakness can be associated with this element and its emotions.

Earth nourishes Metal in the *sheng* cycle. And an efficient digestive process is essential in providing the Lungs and Colon with energy. The principal muscle employed in respiration, the diaphragm, is situated above the digestive organs, which is why we 'breathe into the abdomen' in chi kung, to allow the diaphragm to move freely. Of equal importance to the function of the Lungs, however, is that of the Colon – for without proper digestion via the Earth organs of Stomach/Spleen we would be unable to eliminate waste at all. Metal corresponds to autumn, the season of letting go. And without the harvest, the 'rotting and ripening' of late summer (Earth) this vital process of eliminating old ideas and habits and moving forward with our lives would be impossible.

In the *ke* cycle, meanwhile, Earth controls Water. And without the steadying, rational, common-sense influence of Earth upon Water, we would be paralysed emotionally, overfearful and cautious.

Metal, grief and sorrow

These emotions affect the Lungs and the respiratory system, as well as the skin and the bowels. Conditions include sunken chest, round shoulders, weak voice, frequent colds and flu, asthma and skin complaints such as eczema and all manner of bowel problems, constipation, IBS and more serious complaints such as diverticulitis or Crohn's disease.

Metal nourishes Water in the *sheng* cycle and its clearing and purging influence on our emotional make-up allows us to put an end to periods in our lives that may no longer be productive or appropriate, allowing us a time for rest and contemplation – autumn into winter. Meanwhile in the *ke* cycle Metal controls Wood, enabling us to cut out the 'dead wood' of unrealistic or unsuitable plans. Also, at times of loss, Metal energy can have a moderating influence on the otherwise comparatively destructive emotions of anger associated with the Wood element.

Water, fear and anxiety

These emotions affect the Kidneys and, perhaps more obviously when there is fear, the Bladder. So urinary disease, backache and stiffness, tinnitus, hair loss, chronic anxiety, jealousy and compulsive behaviour and impotence can result.

Water nourishes Wood in the *sheng* cycle, and without the impetus and drive of a healthy Kidney/adrenal complex we cannot possibly begin new ventures. Winter, in other words, can never change into spring and we remain stuck in a rut. In the *ke* cycle, meanwhile, Water controls Fire and without its moderating influence (a little caution is sometimes a good thing) we may become consumed with our desires, wasting lots of time and energy trying to satisfy our emotional needs, often in an inappropriate manner.

All the emotions, as you have seen, are equally valuable and the interaction is constant, reflecting the enormous diversity and richness of the human emotional experience. If a person shuns any emotion or else craves it and strives to experience it constantly, then an internal imbalance is indicated or will shortly develop. Some people crave excitement constantly, while others seek out fear – the Heart and Kidney urging the body on to excess. Violent movies, scary roller-coaster rides or a social life that revolves around endless practical jokes and getting drunk are all ways in which people deal with their negative emotions and try to dissipate them. But these tactics rarely work. The individual, driven on by his or her internal imbalances seeks out more and more stimulation, fright, shock, laughter, whatever, until both body and mind become exhausted. Premature ageing, dependence on stimulants, alcohol, drugs, cigarettes become a way of life, as does a rapid deterioration in health over the years, making it more and more difficult to break free. We become slaves to our emotions, stripped of our liberty and all the glorious potential that each of us is born with. That's how important emotions are.

Getting to grips with those feelings

As you have probably realized by this stage, it is essential to be able to recognize extremes of emotion when they arise and try to deal with them constructively. This should not involve projecting the negativity onto other people, however. Unfortunately, this is something many people often do. They are angry, so they find people to be angry with. They become angry with their family, their neighbours, the government, with people from other cultures or supporters of other football teams. This form of negative energy comes to dominate their existence and what usually happens is that all this anger is simply thrown back at the perpetrator, making matters even worse.

The bottom line is that energy cannot be destroyed, it can only be changed into something else – ideally into something better. And before this can be achieved, we have to focus on the source. We have to look inward. Exploring our feelings with honesty and trying to understand what motivates us in our daily affairs. This is a worthwhile task, because with a little effort we can literally transform negative emotions into a positive vital force –

a vehicle for good, both to ourselves and to others. Let's look at each emotion separately once again and see how this can be achieved.

Exercise for changing anger into kindness

Get in touch with your Wood energy either through visualization and/or by performing the percussive techniques outlined in Chapter 09. If you elect to do visualization, stand or sit quietly for a few moments and picture the location of the Wood energy as it flows around the sides of the head and body, down the sides of the legs, and then up the inside of the legs into the lower chest area (Figure 2, page 9). See this movement of energy and picture it as a soft, green radiance, flowing smoothly. Green is the colour of Wood.

Then start to focus your thoughts on the action of the Wood organs, the Liver and Gall Bladder. The Liver is a storehouse of energy derived from our food and its continual metabolism is what warms our bodies inside. Remember, the Liver also stores the Blood and detoxifies it, especially when we sleep. It prepares nutrients, minerals, vitamins and numerous other chemicals for our use. In fact, the Liver is like a whole separate being in itself, busy with hundreds of different functions, many of them occurring simultaneously. Meanwhile, the Gall Bladder, situated nearby, aids the digestion of fats by storing and secreting bile.

The Liver's own particular kind of emotional energy is called the *Hun*. It is described traditionally as 'the planner; the organizer; the blueprint of who we are'. When the *Hun* is working well, we are able to organize effectively and make decisions – in a sense fulfilling our destiny, whatever that might be. When it is damaged or, in some instances, separated from the body, as can occur, our concept of the future becomes clouded and we drift aimlessly or erratically through life. The Liver and the *Hun*, therefore, are vital to our happiness and to our sense of achievement and fulfilment.

So get in touch with your *Hun* now and with your meditation visualize a brilliant green/blue radiance glowing in the space just behind your lower right ribcage, the location of the Liver. Allow this radiance to extend outwards through all of your body, while at the same time letting go of any feelings of resentment or frustration. See everything as progressing, going forward, evolving and changing, taking you along with it.

Let go of any anger – forgive everyone and everything that has ever held you back or made you sad. Let go of them and their attempts to restrict your liberty and individuality, and simple tell yourself that you are a free spirit, open to change and opportunity. And with that new-found feeling of optimism, think of how much easier it is now going to be to give of yourself, to help others and to be kinder to those you meet – your family, your friends and work colleagues, your community. Realize that all this will flow smoothly and easily, without making any excessive demands on your time or energy unless it is right for you. See the world around you in springtime, full of growth and opportunity, fresh and new. Then breathe deeply into the abdomen for a few moments before finishing your meditation, feeling calm and cheerful.

Exercise for changing excessive joy into peacefulness

Get in touch with your Fire energy either through visualization and/or by performing the percussive techniques outlined in Chapter 09. If you elect to do visualization, stand or sit quietly for a few moments and picture the location of the Fire energy as it flows up and down the centre of the arms, and also along the little finger edge of the arms – into the chest and down to the abdomen and up again (Figure 3, page 9). See this movement of energy and picture it as a soft, crimson radiance flowing smoothly.

Then stand or sit quietly for a few minutes and visualize the action of the heart. The heart is not large – just about the size of a fist, in fact. And although we can usually detect its beat more to the left-hand side in the chest, its actual location is only slightly to the left of centre. The vital task it performs is to act as a double pump, sending blood first to the lungs to pick up oxygen before receiving it back again and then pumping it, still rich with oxygen, all around the body. As we discovered in Chapter 04, the Heart is considered the seat of the mind and ruling spirit in most traditional societies. In China, it is called the *Shen*: an entity that is of prime importance in our emotional lives. The brain, in fact, was not particularly revered by the ancient Chinese physicians who called it, rather unflatteringly, the 'muddy ball'. These days the brain is perhaps better compared to a computer, while the mind (the software and its programmer) resides in some kind of separate space and may possibly be able to survive the death of the brain itself.

One of the most common problems associated with the Heart in this context is when the *Shen* becomes unsettled and restless. This can be due either to shock, to a build-up of stagnant energy and phlegmy material or else from a deficiency in the quality of the Heart Blood itself. Inappropriate mirth, insomnia, forgetfulness, palpitations and a tendency to shout and laugh excessively are symptoms of unbalanced Heart energy. In this case it is said that 'the *Shen* has no residence'. So we must always endeavour to settle the Heart and give the *Shen* its residence.

For your meditation, visualize a soft red radiance glowing in the region of the Heart and, with each exhalation, breathe away any feelings of impatience or agitation that may be lodged there. Allow simple contentment, respect and graciousness to fill this space instead. Realize that genuine happiness and joy can only be built on inner peace and tranquillity. Relax and allow your Heart to fill with compassion for all creatures, including yourself. Learn to love yourself, too – that's important – and to respect what you are able to offer in terms of relationships. Allow your mind to settle into the Heart area and know that here it will reside when you sleep and that your sleep, moreover, will be peaceful and calm. See the world around you as bathing in the warmth and light of summer, with everything growing to maturity and interacting appropriately. Then breathe deeply into the abdomen a few more times before finishing your meditation, feeling calm and cheerful.

Exercise for changing worry into acceptance

Get in touch with your Earth energy either through visualization and/or by performing the percussive techniques outlined in Chapter 09. If you elect to do visualization, stand or sit quietly for a few moments and picture the location of the Earth energy as it flows from the eyes down the face, throat and chest into the abdomen, and then further, down the front aspect of the legs, then up again, returning to the abdomen and chest (Figure 6, page 11). See this movement of energy and picture it as a gentle, golden-yellow radiance, flowing smoothly.

Then stand or sit quietly for a few moments and get in touch with the action of the digestive organs, especially the Spleen and pancreas. As we have seen earlier, the Spleen has a range of functions far beyond that stipulated by the physical organ itself and is considered to play a major part in the digestive process. Together with the pancreas, with which it is arguably synonymous, it also regulates our metabolism, helps to recycle precious blood cells and produces antibodies against disease. For women, the Spleen is also paramount in the understanding of numerous gynaecological complaints. The Spleen is said to hold the Blood in the vessels and this includes the uterus. Heavy, irregular periods, therefore, often have a correlation to a weakened Spleen energy. There is no similarity to this whatsoever in Western physiology, by the way. But for those of us working in the field of oriental medicine the correlation works extremely well in clinical practice.

The form of mental energy associated with the Spleen is called the *Yi*. The *Yi* is associated with our powers of concentration and mental focus, the capacity for applied thinking – such as study. Your *Yi* is probably working overtime right now, reading this book. Students studying long and hard for exams often deplete their Spleen energies – a condition aggravated by poor diet, moreover.

For your meditation, visualize a warm, golden-yellow radiance in the area of the Spleen, just behind the lower part of the left ribcage. Exhale and breathe away any cares and worries, along with any repetitive thoughts that keep running through your mind. Instead, fill the space with feelings of acceptance, that justice and fairness will invariably come to your aid and carry you through any problems you may be facing in the future. Rather than worry about what might happen, resolve now to turn things around so that you can see the situation from the perspective of others and then consider how you can work together with them to establish common values. Keep that golden-yellow glow – the colour of hope and optimism – and realize, too, that the world is a supportive, accommodating and co-operative place, abundant in its gifts and favours. See the harvest being gathered in – it is late summer and the days are warm and sensuous, full of peace and contentment. Breathe deeply into the abdomen a few more times before finishing your meditation, feeling calm and cheerful.

Exercise for changing grief into 'letting go'

Get in touch with your Metal energy either through visual-ization and/or by performing the percussive techniques outlined in Chapter 9. If you elect to do visualization, stand or sit quietly for a few moments and picture the location of the Metal energy as it flows from the chest down the thumb side of the arm and then back up again into the throat and face and also descending deeply inside, down to the lower abdomen (Figure 4, page 10). See this movement of energy and picture it as a clear, white radiance, flowing smoothly.

For your visualization, stand or sit quietly for a few minutes and get in touch with the location of the lungs, in the chest, either side of the centre line and extending also towards the back of the body. The lungs are quite large organs, which receive the air from outside and then transfer this to the blood via the pumping action of the heart. They also filter out waste products from the blood at the same time, such as carbon dioxide – which is then exhaled. The Lungs have an effect on the skin and our levels of perspiration, as well.

The particular kind of mental energy associated with the Lungs is called the *Po*. This is thought to be that part of us which 'feels' in an emotional sense. It represents vigorous life force in all its guises. It is extremely sensitive and can suffer very easily through sadness and grief. If this is the case, then the entire respiratory system and the skin can suffer. Excessive nostalgia or not wanting to let go of the past is a prime symptom of a distressed *Po*. If you translate this in terms of the action of the Colon it is like a kind of mental constipation, which can also have a powerful physical correlation in the workings of the lungs as well as the bowels. Like the Colon, which excretes waste matter, the Lungs are also organs of elimination – in this case, eliminating carbon dioxide and other toxins from the blood via exhalation or else from the surface of the skin. The skin is often described as 'the third lung' – and diseases of the skin, such as eczema or psoriasis are often stress related or aggravated by feelings of loss or sadness. This can occur at a very early age, moreover and many cases of childhood eczema can be traced to emotional upsets.

For your meditation, imagine a brilliant white light glowing in the lungs, particularly as you inhale, filling the lungs with vitality and brightness. The lungs feel softer and moist, expanding and contracting freely within the chest cavity. Then see all that energy circulating around the body with the blood, reaching to every cell, nourishing it and replenishing it with vitality and oxygen. See the skin glowing radiantly and the colon energized also, ready to move any waste matter along and through. Then, with the exhalation, breathe away any feelings of grief or sorrow – and see a dull, smoky cloud escaping and drifting away into the air. Breathe away all negative emotion, all sadness, depression – let it all go with that out-breath. Then breathe in again and fill your body with light.

See the season of autumn, golden and crisp, the leaves falling, nature letting go of the old. Know that you too can let go when need be. You can let go in order to be renewed. Allow feelings of gladness and acceptance to fill your mind with each inhalation. Then breathe deeply into the abdomen a few more times before finishing your meditation, feeling calm and cheerful.

Exercise for changing fear into motivation

Get in touch with your Water energy either through visualization and/or by performing the percussive techniques outlined in Chapter 09. If you elect to do visualization, stand or sit quietly for a few moments and picture the location of the Water energy as it flows from the inner corners of the eyes, over the head, down the back, the buttocks and the back of the legs, then up from the soles of the feet, through the abdomen, either side of the breastbone to the throat again (Figure 5, page 11). See this movement of energy and picture it as a bright blue radiance, flowing smoothly.

Then stand or sit quietly for a few minutes and visualize the action of the Kidneys and their adrenal glands, powering the body ahead, producing hormones and other chemicals that help the body mobilize itself for action and also deal with wounds and inflammation. The Kidneys are the body's great filtering system. Around 1200 millilitres of blood pass through the two kidneys every minute. During this time, the kidneys remove impurities from the blood stream and also help to regulate the precise amount of internal fluids we should have in our body. This regulates the blood quantity and also the blood pressure. Any excess fluid, meanwhile, is excreted by the associated yang organ, the Bladder.

The mental aspect of the Kidneys is called the *Zhi*. This is traditionally described as will power and the striving towards targets and goals. It links in very nicely with the other correspondences of the Water element such as impetus and drive. When the *Zhi* is functioning properly, we have the energy and the will to undertake things and see them through. When out of balance, however, fear and anxiety take over and we simply lack the will to make any of the right moves in life at all!

For your meditation, visualize two areas of brilliant blue radiance in the small of the back, either side of the spine at about waist level. See these areas radiating their energy up and down either side of the spine, up over the head and down into the eyes and also down the back of the legs into the feet. See the Kidneys cleansing the blood and taking away all impurities. Breathe out and observe through your mind's eye any anxieties or fears being cleansed away and a sense of motivation and invention taking their place. Know that you can achieve whatever you set out to do, that you have the inner resources to make it happen! Know that the potential, like a potent seed, is there, waiting for you to animate it at any time.

Picture in your mind's eye the cool winter landscape, calm and mysterious, full of hidden seed and latent energy, rich with potential, just waiting to burst forth into life. Picture the power and strength of Water, too. See the ocean, deep, mysterious, full of strength and energy. Breathe deeply into the abdomen a few more times before finishing your meditation, feeling calm and cheerful.

Cultivating detachment

Succeeding in meditations like these depends on how well we can cultivate a sense of detachment from our emotions. In other words, it is sometimes helpful to view negative emotions as existing independently of ourselves. So, for instance, you could say to yourself that, 'there is anger', rather than, 'I am angry', 'there is fear', rather than 'I am anxious and afraid'. There is a great difference between these two types of statements. Regular chi kung practice, even simply the physical movements themselves, enables us to cultivate a sense of calm and emotional balance, but we sometimes need to help this on its way through a positive mental approach and by reminding ourselves that it is possible to have control over our emotions. This is a very liberating experience – simply to know that it is possible to break free from time to time, to take charge of our feelings and to alter them into something more positive.

Meditation: the building of chi

The space between Heaven and Earth is like a bellows.

Tao Te Ching

We are now going to look at a simple all-round meditation technique that has been used for thousands of years by those practising chi kung and Taoist philosophy, as well as by martial artists and by practitioners of oriental medicine. It goes by various names, but the one I like best is 'The Union of *Li* and *K'an*' – or the Union of Fire and Water. This works on the movement and generation of chi through the *tan tien* centre that we touched on briefly in earlier chapters, but here we are going to enhance this energy and focus it more strongly by moving it in a continuous cycle up from the lower abdomen to the solar plexus, then back down again, guided by the breath. This is repeated over and over until a sensation of energy or warmth is felt in the *tan tien* (which lies between these two areas, of course). This is often explained in terms of Water below the *tai tien* in the lower abdomen and Fire above, in the solar plexus area. Metaphorically speaking, this mixing of Fire (*Li*) with water (*K'an*) produces 'steam' – the chi.

There are several interesting parallels between this exercise and those outlined in other disciplines such as yoga and meditation. In each case, the practitioner is seeking to redirect or to convert the more base energies, for instance the sexual energies, into more refined and health-giving properties – something that, rather than being wasted through elimination, ejaculation (in men) or menstruation (in women), is directed into a form of energy that the body can use more constructively.

Now this isn't exactly a difficult concept to grasp, but many people upon hearing it are immediately alarmed by the idea of having to tamper with their sexual energies. After all, most people are quite happy with their sexual energies. Don't worry! Nobody has to suddenly convert to a life of celibacy in order to practise this meditation or to derive the benefits from it. All that is required is to divert a little spare energy elsewhere in the body. This comes as a great relief to most students when they realize this. And when they also hear that it can actually enhance their sexual energies and boost their performance ... well, it is amazing how quickly they change their mind about the whole procedure! 'Give us the Union of *Li* and *K'an*' they cry. Let's get started right away!

Getting started

Sexual energies, as most of us know, tend to be focused below the navel, in fact quite low down in the pubic region. This has always been described in oriental culture as the region of Water or *K'an* – an abstract, almost psychic quality that embraces the idea of depth, hidden potential and also therefore includes the concept of the *Jing*. Located a little way beneath the *tan tien* centre, it is also referred to in classic texts such as the *I Ching* as the 'Seat of Water' and also, elsewhere, compared to the moon and the season of winter. Above the *tan tien*, meanwhile, we have what is called *Li* – which means Fire. This area, actually just beneath the heart, corresponds to the solar plexus and is referred to as the 'Seat of Fire' in the *I Ching* and compared to the sun and to the season of summer. In the same scheme of things, Fire and Water are also often compared to heaven and earth respectively – in other words two great archetypal principles are being described here, representing that which is above and that which is below. Yang and yin.

These energy centres (called psychic centres sometimes, since they are obviously not discernible on a physical level) are used extensively in Taoist and yogic meditation, and they play an important role in the movement of energy from the lower centres to the higher faculties – i.e. brain, spirit, call it what you will. The difference here is that we are looking at a constant back and forth interchange of chi, like a small circulation of energy, up and down, building up a conscious strength and vigour in the *tan tien*. Here's how.

Li and *K'an*: the meditation

Go back again to your standing posture, described in Chapter 08, and once you feel comfortable begin to visualize the breath building in the abdomen. On the next convenient inhalation, lift your energy up from the lower abdomen, by guiding it not only with your mind but by raising the hands. The hands in this instance are palms up, as if supporting a large ball or balloon. Make sure the hands are relaxed, the fingers slightly separated and curvaceous, no sharp angles. Raise the hands and bring them up as high as the solar plexus, *Li*, the Seat of Fire, just below where the ribs meet in the centre.

Then, as the subsequent exhalation comes along, rotate the wrists, so that the palms face downward, as if resting on the top of the balloon this time, and then lower them back down to the *tan tien* and beyond, towards the lower abdomen and the Seat of Water once again. This completes one whole cycle, which you then begin over again straight away with the next inhalation, raising the hands up from *K'an* to *Li*, and so on. Add more and more visualization to the movement once you are totally familiar and comfortable with it. Try to cultivate that perception of fire coming down to water and of water rising up to meet fire – always raising chi upwards as you breathe in and then sending it downwards again as you breathe out. Remember this upwards and downwards movement should be visualized as mixing, circulating, combining Fire with Water. The resulting vapour builds as chi in the *tan tien* itself, beneath the navel. See it happening, like a gently bubbling caldron (an image often used in this process), growing stronger, warmer, more vibrational.

On a purely practical level, this meditation is a remarkably effective way to produce a quick-fix relaxation. At any time when you are experiencing stress or pressure, just go through this meditation, using the hand movements described and you will feel calmer almost immediately. Do it for a minute or two and you will become deeply relaxed.

Active chi kung with *Li* and *K'an*

Clearly the more passive Standing like a Tree posture is ideal for this kind of meditation, but you can also work this energy up and down and into the limbs as well. And for this, the moving chi kung exercises that we looked at in the earlier chapters of this book are ideal. So, once you have gone some way towards experiencing the sensation of chi circulating in the abdomen, try to imagine the chi flowing in a more general sense along the arms and legs. Send it there with your breathing. This then takes your chi kung experience onto a different level entirely in which the chi is raised with the inhalation, often out into the arms and then drawn back and lowered again on the exhalation. Each individual chi kung exercise is different, of course, and has its own characteristics of chi movement. But the principle is the same, the chi moves with the breath and so does the body.

To put this into practical terms, let's revisit each one of the exercises again briefly and see how each one can accommodate this kind of movement and circulation in its own right.

The Big Breath (Chapter 03)

With the opening of the arms and the inhalation, guide the chi up from *K'an* to *Li*. Then as you exhale and lower the palms, guide the chi down again through the mid-line to the *tan tien* or below. The next inhalation naturally brings chi up again from *K'an* to *Li*, and so on. Repeat this cycle, co-ordinating the movement of chi to your breathing.

With time, you can start to bring the sensation of chi right up into the arms as you inhale – almost drawing it up from the earth through the soles of your feet, up the mid-line of the body and out along as far as the thumbs. Don't forget to bring it back down again as you exhale. Chi should never be allowed to become 'stuck' in the upper part of the body.

Three Burners (Chapter 04)

With each inhalation, and as you open up the arm to the side, guide the chi upwards from *K'an* to *Li*. Then, as you exhale and the hand comes back in again, lower the chi back down to the *tan tien*. This is done three times, of course. Then with the overhead movement and extension of the arm, allow the energy to extend right out along the limb. With the final exhalation, guide the chi back down the centre into the *tan tien* once more. Repeat this cycle, co-ordinating the movement of chi to your breathing.

Don't neglect your Triple Burner visualization, however. Remember you are harmonizing the three spaces with the movement of your hand each time you open and close. Think of the energy rising up a little higher each time. Hand, elbow and shoulder level. Bring it down again at the conclusion of the exercise.

Drawing the Bow (Chapter 05)

As you raise the hands at the commencement of this movement, guide the chi up from *K'an* to *Li*. Then as you extend the arm you can diffuse it more into the tendons of the arm itself. You take at least one whole breath while holding the extended arm position, in which you can breathe the energy up once more into the upper body on the inhalation and then out and along the arm again with the exhalation. Then, with the final exhalation, and as you lower the arms, guide the chi back down to the *tan tien* once again. Repeat as you Draw the Bow to the other side, co-ordinating the movement of chi to your breathing.

Ripples in the Stream (Chapter 06)

This is an opportunity to circulate chi around what is called the *dai mai*, or belt channel. As we have seen this is the only acu-channel that is not longitudinal – that is, not running along the length of the body or the limbs, but around the waist, like a belt or girdle. Simply guide the chi around, in a circle, with the movements of your hands – forward and out on the inhalation, around and back with the exhalation. Imagine the chi from the *tan tien* circulating around the waist in a broad band, taking in the pelvic region in the front and the kidneys in the back as it goes. Move the chi (and the hands, too, of course) with the breath.

You can also visualize energy rising up on the in-breath from the soles of your feet where a major acu-point called the Bubbling Spring is located, remember? (See page 89.) This will help nourish your Kidney energy and strengthen the legs.

Squeezing the Ball (Chapter 07)

There is not a great amount of movement of the hands here to guide the chi for you, so you really need to summon up your powers of visualization to the full. That said, however, if you do the more advanced version of this movement described in Chapter 07, in which you very slightly raise the hands with the inhalation and lower them with the exhalation, you will have a physical correlation for raising the chi up from *K'an* to *Li* each time, that works particularly well.

To put this another way, as you inhale and allow the ball to push your hands apart, you draw the chi upwards to *Li*, and then – as you squeeze the ball and exhale – you guide it downwards again to the *tan tien*.

That concludes our brief look at the emotions and meditation. There is a lot of material here and it is recommended that you spend some weeks working slowly through it. There is more to both these subjects, of course, much more than can possibly be described in this small book. And in a sense, each person will experience these exercises in their own way and derive different insights and ideas from them as they progress. This is why chi kung is, at heart, an intensely personal experience. And the exploration of these experiences takes us yet another step further on our journey of discovery, into the world of ideas and philosophy. This, in fact, is precisely where we are going to next. But just before we go, here is a final look at the Five Elements once again, with many of their attributes and correspondences listed in table form.

Wood	Fire	Earth	Metal	Water
Spring	Summer	Late Summer	Autumn	Winter
Germination	Growth	Ripening	Harvest	Storage
East	South	Centre	West	North
Wind	Heat	Dampness	Dryness	Cold
Green	Red	Yellow	White	Black/Blue
Liver	Heart	Spleen	Lungs	Kidneys
Eyes	Tongue	Mouth	Nose	Ears
Anger	Elation	Pensiveness	Grief	Fear
Shouting	Laughing	Singing	Weeping	Groaning
Forest	Heath	Fields	Clouds	Rivers/Sea
Life	Sunshine	Soil	Minerals	Rainfall
Creativity	Inspiration	Common Sense	Melancholy	Contemplation

table 5 attributes of the Five Elements

chi kung and philosophy

In this chapter you will learn:
- about the philosophy of Taoism
- about the importance of detachment and 'letting go'
- about advanced practice and the use of chi kung in daily life.

By doubting we may question, and by questioning we may come to know the truth.

Abelard

Now, some people, when confronted by the word philosophy, either run or hide. Whether this is something to do with memories of school or college, conjuring up images of dusty old books stacked high on desks and shelves, with equally dusty old people moving mysteriously among them, is not always clear. But run they do and hide they must, until it's all over, until the philosopher passes on, the books are put away and people start talking sense again and we can all get on with the more pressing and vitally important activities of life ... like shopping!

Philosophy is important, however. And if you intend to study anything like chi kung seriously you need to have at least a passing acquaintance with this venerable old way of looking at 'life, the universe and everything'. It is an essential part of your mental kit, because fundamentally philosophy is all about asking questions and this reveals a mind that is inevitably trying to change and evolve. Curiosity may have killed the cat, but it did at least indicate a glimmer of feline intelligence in motion at the time.

Children, of course, are forever asking questions – it's part of the growing up process. But in time we become more settled and our curiosity becomes blunted. Therein lies the danger. Because the moment we stop asking questions our internal energies begin to stagnate. Life holds no surprises for us, no magic, because we already 'know it all'. This can occur at a remarkably early age, moreover. Most teenagers already 'know it all'. Later, if they are very fortunate they might realize, sometime during their early twenties perhaps, that they do not, after all, quite know *everything* and can then start to ask questions once more and progress to a further stage of development. This marks the start of real maturity – spring into summer, to use the symbolism we met with in the last chapter. In this way, each person will eventually find in their chosen philosophy – for we all develop a philosophy of some kind eventually – a way of making sense of his or her own life and, hopefully, of finding some measure of peace and contentment in the process. And of all the many different philosophical systems at large, the one we must inevitably consider if we practise chi kung to any level or standard is called *Taoism*.

The tao in Taoism

The word *Tao* (pronounced as *dao* by the way) has been variously translated as 'the way', 'the path' or 'the spirit'. In this, it is worth reminding ourselves that the word 'spirit' has nothing to do with ghosts or spooks or people sitting on clouds, but actually comes from a Latin root which means 'breath'. So although translations of this kind take us close to an understanding of the word *Tao*, none is entirely satisfactory. In fact, the *Tao* itself cannot really be put into words, because language itself is far too limiting. The classic text of Taoism, the *Tao Te Ching*, composed around the sixth century BCE, and about which we will have much to say shortly, puts it very neatly:

> *The Tao that can be told is not the eternal Tao.*
> *The name that can be named is not the eternal name.*

Perhaps we are being told here that we cannot penetrate to reality through words or even through thoughts alone, but only by direct experience. Thoughts and ideas tend to get in the way, in fact. This is also something those participating in chi kung will understand full well. Chi flows easily where there is least resistance and one of the greatest barriers to chi flow is the existence of fixed ideas. Unfortunately most of us come complete with a whole lot of preconceptions and fixed ideas and other personal baggage gathered from our past, most of it superfluous to needs. This is where Taoism comes in. Taoism is about letting go of fixed ideas, of making space inside and allowing things to happen spontaneously. That's how it helps us let go of all that mental baggage. There is a kind of chicken and egg situation here moreover, because although you need something like Taoism to help develop your chi kung, you will also find that one of the best ways to approach the study of Taoism is through something practical and physical – like chi kung itself. The one feeds off and supports the other, just like any true yin/yang combination.

In other words, as you progress with your chi kung exercises and explore the sensations and feelings that arise, you will discover, too, that the more you can relax in any field of endeavour, not just chi kung but *anywhere* – at work or at play – the easier life itself becomes. Think for a moment about what you have learned so far in this book. Sure, we all have to work hard in the early stages of assimilating any new movement or technique, but these exercises are fairly straightforward and thereafter it is all down to practice, and lots of it. Then we just need to relax into the movements, to let go of all those thoughts. The less hard we try, the easier it becomes and the more lasting the results. This is one of the key Taoist concepts – flexibility and adaptability in life, and of simply allowing things to take their course. This, in a very real sense, can be a matter of survival.

An army without flexibility never wins a battle.
A tree, unbending, is easily broken.

Tao Te Ching

The art of spontaneity

In Taoist thinking, unlike its rival philosophy in ancient China, Confucianism, we find a bold rejection of formality and regulation. In its place comes a refreshing originality and simplicity – a celebration of innocence and spontaneity that allows the individual to respond to challenges calmly without trying to meet them aggressively head on. This avoidance of confrontation and the notion of easy movement without effort is ideally suited to the thought process underlying chi kung as it surely is for all those engaged in the Taoist arts, be it philosophy, medicine, martial arts, calligraphy or poetry, where the experience of spontaneous action and the union of yang and yin must occur without the obstruction of too much conscious analysis. Stop thinking – let it happen! That's the way.

This minimalist ideal – rather in vogue at the present time in certain areas such as interior design – is frequently expressed in the Taoist texts as 'letting go of the need to do things'. By making space for the essentials in life, we are told, the essentials will be done. There is much to be gained by applying these principles daily, for the advantages thus gained can reach right out to all of our affairs and duties.

In the pursuit of learning, every day something is acquired
In the pursuit of the Tao, every day something is dropped
... When nothing is done, nothing is left undone.

Tao Te Ching

So once again, we find that Taoism is all about shedding limitations, emptying ourselves of tensions, of second-hand beliefs, political dogma, greed and jealousy. We do not limit ourselves in any sense by pursuing what is irrelevant, but instead 'open up' and renew each day the vast potential of life that lies before us. In this way, everything becomes possible and 'nothing is left undone'.

Doesn't make sense!

Now, some people don't like this sort of thing. They would say it doesn't make sense, that it's impractical. 'How can you get things done by not doing them?' they ask and not without good reason. There's an obvious contradiction here, yes – but Taoism is actually all about contradictions and of actually embracing the inconsistencies of life. Perhaps the best way to understand this is to think of all those times when you tried so hard to do things and still you didn't get them done! Then when you simply relaxed, hey presto! there was suddenly space enough for the solution to appear. *Making space* is what Taoism is all about. Letting the creative energies flow. Then all things are possible.

For those who are still in the dark, however, and who really do prefer lists, try the following for size. In trying to understand the Taoist attitude to life, certainly the following principles need to be considered.

- Respect for the natural world.
- Respect for the individual.
- Belief that simplicity is better than complexity.
- Belief that yielding is better than confrontation.
- Belief that tyranny and violence are wrong and damaging.
- Belief that it is better to inspire others than to coerce.
- Belief that true leadership comes only through service and humility.
- Belief that life is a journey and that change is inevitable in all things.
- Belief that energy flows through all things and is shared by all things.

For all that lists of this kind are helpful, it still has to be stressed that Taoism remains and always will remain a philosophy without strict rules or laws. And if you managed to find still more contradictions within that list, all well and good. Life is full of them. And this is why Taoism does not seek to impose its will on the world or upon others; it does not assert itself or glorify itself or take up extreme positions; and it does not even insist that its ways are correct. Rather, it tries to work with nature, with all its diversity and contradictions, to contemplate the interdependence of all things and to cultivate a sense of inner peace and humility as a result.

Essentially, therefore, the *Tao* is something that has to be experienced with the mind or heart, rather than the intellect. It is all around us if we care to look and we are in touch with it always because every living thing has its own smaller, more personal *tao* – written with a small 't' – its own path or self-selected purpose in life. By working on our own energies and

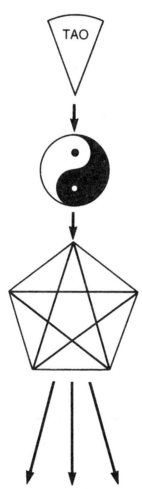

figure 49 experiencing the Tao

thoughts, by reconciling the Five Elements in all their diversity, and by bringing together the opposing forces of yang and yin in our body and mind, there is every chance that this, our individual tao, can become part of the greater, universal *Tao*. That is an ideal, of course. But there is nothing wrong with ideals. And even if we achieve it only momentarily, it is well worth the effort (Figure 49).

Lao Tsu – the old teacher

It is clear from the oldest classical texts from ancient China, that Taoist ideas existed way back in the mists of time, even long before its greatest exponent, the legendary sage Lao Tsu, wrote them down in the great classic of Chinese literature, the *Tao Te Ching* – written around the sixth century BCE. This is a book well worth studying, by the way, if you wish to pursue these ideas in more depth. One of the great literary works of antiquity and still relevant today, it draws the reader back again and again to its pages – with always something new to offer, always something fresh.

Lao Tsu is rather a difficult figure to pin down in an historical sense and some scholars even dispute his existence. The name Lao Tsu literally means 'the old sage', or 'the old teacher' and it is possible that the work that bears this name is a compilation from several authors, perhaps even those writing at different periods. At any rate there is, in my view, a remarkable consistency and unity of ideas running through the whole work, which strongly suggests the hand of one person, with perhaps just a few additions or annotations over time. None of this really matters, of course, because the main point of interest for us is that the *Tao Te Ching* is a literary masterpiece; it represents the philosophy of Taoism in its essence. Its tidy, succinct aphorisms, some only a few lines in length have been translated into all the major languages of the world and it is today probably more widely read than ever before.

But to return to the legend ... Lao Tsu is said to have held the prestigious post of archivist at the Imperial Court in China around the sixth century BCE. In his old age, when retirement was beckoning, he set out alone towards the remote western borders of China, perhaps wishing to escape the turbulent world of courtly intrigue and politics and to lead the simple life, who knows! But when he reached the border post, the gatekeeper suggested that Lao Tsu, being such a renowned philosopher, should commit his ideas and thoughts to paper before he and his knowledge passed on through the gateway and into the wilderness.

He is then said to have composed in some 5000 characters of text the *Tao Te Ching* which, translated into English is sometimes referred to as 'The Way and its Power'. And although at various stages of its history the *Tao Te Ching* and the teachings of Lao Tsu have become entangled in political affairs and also a fair smattering of superstition, with just about everybody and anybody at some stage seeing in its abstract quality something to justify their own possibly quite quirky views, its core teaching remains unchanged, and still of outstanding quality and value.

The heroic quest

Perhaps the reason why the story of the *Tao Te Ching* and its creation has endured for so long is because it encapsulates three essential features of Taoist thought. First, that it is a vivid sketch of an individual and his life's experiences – and Taoism prizes individuality highly. Second, that it involves a journey, away from the complexity of the metropolis towards the simplicity of the wilderness; and the Tao itself is often referred to as a pathway, a journey towards a less complex, more naive and lucid mental state. And third, that it involves a transition, through the gates into a different phase of existence or, to put it another way, a different state of consciousness, something which is essential in order to realize some measure of enlightenment.

In this way we are reminded of the archetypal heroic quest so prevalent in mythology and legend, from the voyage of Odysseus in Homeric Greece to the Arthurian legends of medieval Europe. To identify with this quest is a personal thing, the individual's own journey towards self-discovery. And perhaps this is why Taoism cannot really ever be taught; it can only be experienced. The role of a teacher, according to Taoist ideals, is therefore simply to guide – as all good teachers do, of course, of whatever persuasion.

Chi kung, Taoism – these are all further steps along the way. And in a sense, by reading this book and putting the exercises you have found here into practice, you have already embarked on that journey – or have at least taken another valuable step. You have already developed an understanding for the harmony of opposites – the yang and the yin of nature. You have already looked at the way matter and energy interchange constantly through contemplation of the Five Elements. And you have, I hope, felt in a very real sense by now the existence of an energy that is all at once both within you and outside you and which flows through all things. Congratulations might be in order here!

Exercise for the circulation of energy

We are now going to turn our attention to another special kind of 'journey', a meditation prized by the Taoist for centuries. There are many variations on this technique – probably as many as there are currently masters teaching it. But generally it develops from the earlier union of *Li* and *K'an* that we looked at in the last chapter, into what is called the Circulation of Energy. In essence, this is the movement of chi around the whole body through the acu-channels that run along the mid-line of the back and mid-line of the front aspect of the torso and head. This kind of meditation was pursued by the ancient philosophers and alchemists of China and there is much mystery and confusion surrounding its purpose. For us today, however, it remains a wonderful mechanism for transforming negative energy and negative emotions, for stimulating the organs and endocrine system and for promoting a greater awareness of the movement of chi within the body.

Attainment of this circulation is both simple and difficult. (There's a typical piece of Taoism contradiction for you!) It is simple in the sense that the energy is already flowing through the channels all the while anyway, otherwise we would not be alive. The difficulty comes from the fact that with this exercise we are seeking to enhance this flow and to circulate it much more freely.

The passive chi kung postures such as Standing like a Tree described in Chapter 08 or Squeezing the Ball from Chapter 07 are ideally suited for this meditation. You can also do it seated – preferably in a straight backed chair or else in either the cross-legged lotus or Japanese *seiza* position (kneeling and sitting on heels). The meditation itself is variously called 'Building the Bridge', 'The Bridge of Magpies', 'The Small Heavenly circulation' or – rather confusingly 'The Large Heavenly Circulation' – and probably many other names, for that matter. Here, we will simply call it the Circulation of Energy.

Like so many exercises and items of special knowledge from the East, this circulation technique was until quite recently understood by only a few – although medical practitioners in China have always been aware of it, of course, since numerous acupuncture points are located along these channels – and some martial artists as well have employed it in their training. Otherwise, it was rarely discussed or written about except in allegorical terms. This is because it also had, and still does have, associations with Chinese alchemy and magical practices. The term magic has had a rather bad press in China during various periods of its history. Just as here in the West, it has often been associated with superstition and ignorance. It's worth bearing in mind, however, that the word 'magic' is often something outsiders apply merely to the demonstration of unusual powers and abilities, something beyond their experience and understanding. The Circulation of Energy can bestow increased abilities in whatever way you choose – in healing, in martial applications, in sexual activities, whatever. In the process, it can seem unusual, and it can appear strange – but it is not magic. It is simply the result of lots of study and hard work.

You have, in a sense, already begun in the earlier chapters of this book to enhance this circulation during the visualization techniques suggested for the physical exercises. You have visualized the Union of Water and Fire in the abdomen and also, during the Standing like a Tree posture, seen how each breath taken into the *tan tien* helps to stoke up the embers of chi in that area, while the out-breath provides the opportunity to spread the energy out all over the body. That's fine. But what we want to do now is channel this energy more effectively.

The Bridge of Magpies

What we are interested in are the two major acu-channels that flow along the mid-line of the body, front and back. The one which runs up the back is called the *Du* channel, or *Du Mai*, while that which runs down the front is called the *Ren* channel, or *Ren Mai*. The *Du* is considered primarily a yang channel, with yang energy coursing through it, while the *Ren* is yin.

Both the *Du Mai* and the *Ren Mai* have their origins in the lower abdomen, but emerge together and flow to the surface at the perineum. The perineum is the lowest part of the body, where the legs join the trunk, just behind the genitals, therefore. Now, with the *Du* channel flowing up the spine, over the head and down to the nose and the *Ren* channel flowing up the mid-line of the front of the body to the throat, the two channels naturally converge again at the mouth. This is a place where many other acu-channels meet and join, by the way, a place which is sometimes called 'the bridge'. The symbolism of the bridge is of particular significance, since the connection between the *Du* and *Ren* channels is slightly imperfect at this place, with numerous minor branches of energy fanning out. What we are seeking to achieve with this exercise is, in part, to build a better bridge between the *Du* and *Ren* channels. When this happens the energy of the body can mix and flow more efficiently and is therefore able to nourish all the organs, vessels and bones of the body far more effectively than before, bringing great benefits in terms of health. It is also thought that the endocrine system or hormonal glands of the body are stimulated more effectively once this circuit is enhanced, since the glands themselves are all situated on route, close to the mid-line.

Preparation

In the Standing like a Tree posture outlined in Chapter 08, or else sitting comfortably in a straight-backed chair, lightly touch the tip of your tongue to the roof of your mouth. Place it just behind the upper front teeth as if saying the letter 'l', but keep it there. The jaw should relax and your mouth might even open very slightly as you do this, but make sure the air continues to be inhaled and exhaled through your nose. This placement of the tongue helps to unite the *Du* and *Ren* channels and enhances the interchange of energy between them – far more efficiently than would normally be the case. If saliva builds up, swallow it. It is considered beneficial and you should never be disturbed if more saliva seems to be forming in your mouth when you do this work.

Directions

1

Breathe in and energize the *tan tien* centre beneath the navel according to the suggestions outlined in earlier chapters. You can think of an ember glowing brightly, as if fanned by bellows or visualize a small furnace – whatever appeals to your imagination. Sometimes it feels a bit like the sensation of 'butterflies' in a nervous tummy. The main thing is to generate the sensation of energy and vitality in that area. It may take a while. Use *Li* and *K'an* if you wish. Be patient.

Tips

With all this extra concentration, don't forget your posture. The base of the spine, the sacrum, is tucked in gently, as is the chin, so that the whole of the spinal column, including the neck appears to lengthen. The point of suspension at the crown of the head is also visualized. The breath is directed downwards into the abdomen, using diaphragm breathing. If you are in the Standing like a Tree posture, keep those knees soft and the arms held out from the body, the elbows a little below the level of the hands. The arms themselves should continue to present a pleasing roundness to their shape, with no sharp angles at the elbows or wrists.

2

When you feel you have built up some chi in the *tan tien*, breathe out and visualize this warmth or energy descending down to the perineum. It may be difficult at first to keep the sensation of energy there at first, but keep trying. Breathe it downwards.

3

At this stage things start to really get interesting, because you begin to make use of a much maligned and neglected part of your anatomy that goes by numerous unflattering names and is the object of endless innuendoes among would-be comedians – the anus. Yes, your anus is now going to be the focus of your attention! From one of the most humble parts of the body comes the opportunity of ascending to the heights – literally, since you are going to use the anus to help 'pump' the chi up along the pathway of the *du* channel that runs along the centre of the back.

With the chi collected at the area of the perineum, breathe in and then contract the sphincter muscles of the anus. Imagine this is acting as a pump to push the chi up into the spine and then higher, as high as you can.

Tips

Ultimately you are trying to pump this extra chi flow right up to the crown of the head, but it will almost certainly take more than one breath for you to experience anything even remotely like this. Even after a great deal of effort and anus crunching, you might still only experience the chi rising to the mid-back or the neck. This means that you simply have to stoke up some more energy in the *tan tien* and send it round and up again to reinforce what is already there, using that sacral pump still and lots of visualization to aid the process. Masters of chi kung will variously describe places where the chi can become stuck during this journey. These include the small of the back, between the shoulder blades and the base of the skull. One of the best ways to aid the passage of chi through these areas is to keep the spine straight as just described. You know the techniques well by now: sacrum tucked under, chin tucked in, scapular rounded and so on.

One more important point: in the very unlikely event that you ever experience any unpleasant sensations during this or any other meditation technique that seeks to raise energy upwards, simply stop straight away and draw the energy back down again to the abdomen. You can do this easily and quickly by breathing out and guiding the chi down mentally and also by using your hands, 'pushing' the chi down with a downward movement of your palms in front of your chest (see pages 145–6) and use the *Li* to *K'an* techniques that you have already learned. Do this several times if necessary. It settles the chi back down again to the *tan tien*.

4

With the possible sensation of increased energy flow at the top of the spine and head, and with the tip of your tongue still in contact with the roof of your mouth, exhale and visualize the chi flowing from the roof of the mouth down to the root of the tongue, so the chi is able to flow from the *Du* into the *Ren* channel. Note that the root of the tongue lies right at the back of the throat – much further back than most people realize, in fact.

Tips

You can, of course, only achieve this if the tongue remains in place, lightly touching the upper palate throughout. It is difficult at first to know exactly where it should be touching the palate, so experiment until you find somewhere which feels in some sense different from the surrounding tissue. It may feel like a slight hollow, accommodating the tip of the tongue or it may feel like a tingling, electrical kind of spot, different from the surrounding tissue; alternatively it may feel hot, or cold, or unusually dry. Everyone may have a different perception of this spot, but once you do locate it, you *will* know. For my part, when it first happened, it felt as if my tongue had grown several inches longer and was protruding right up into my head! This, however, may not be your perception. Be ready for something, anything that feels appreciably different to warrant attention, and then home in on that.

5

The chi is now passing down through the bridge you have made in the mouth and into the throat. The next inhalation, therefore, constitutes the start of the whole process again. This time, however, you are inhaling not only the new air chi down into the abdomen, but also the circulated chi from the previous cycle. All together, send the energy down once more to the *tan tien* centre beneath the navel, where the furnace is further activated and yet more chi is prepared for its tour of the body (down to the perineum, up the spine and so on). You have now enhanced your natural energy flow at least to some degree and made a vital connection between the yang and yin circulation within your body and mind. Well done!

Tips

As mentioned in the previous chapter, at the very end of your session, it's always a good idea to finish up by focusing the energy back into the *tan tien* area. Always make sure you draw energy down, never up, at the conclusion of your exercise.

Going further with the chi

Once you have some sensation, no matter how meagre, of energy circulating through these channels, you might like to experiment in ways to extend it beyond the mid-line circuit – for example into the limbs. Different systems teach their own variations on this theme. Here is one suggestion that is fairly 'main stream' in chi kung terms.

Once the central, mid-line orbit is established, bring the energy up the *Du Mai* in the usual manner, breathing in. When it reaches the shoulder blades, send it down the outside of the arms, on the exhalation, then up the inside of the arms as you breathe in again. You can let it cross sides, if you wish, from one arm to the next.

With the energy returning to the spine, breathe in and raise it to the top of the head. Then with the subsequent exhalation, allow the energy to descend through the tongue and throat down to the *tan tien* once more.

From here to the perineum again and then, on the out-breath, down the outside of the legs to the feet.

On the subsequent in-breath, draw the energy back from the soles of the feet (Bubbling Spring) and up the inside of the legs to the perineum once more.

At this point you can either go back to the *tan tien* or around and up the spine again and down the arms, and so on – repeating as many times as you wish.

This inclusion of the limbs in the meditation is often described as the Greater Heavenly Circulation. It is something extremely difficult to achieve to any great degree and is a lifetime goal for even the most diligent of chi kung practitioners. Most people – and I include myself here – will have only a fleeting experience of it, if at all. So, in other words, do not be in the least bit discouraged if you cannot feel anything strong or terribly convincing with this exercise straight away or even after a few months of practice. Simply to make the mental effort, to imagine it happening, is possibly quite valuable in its own right as it reinforces a strong mental image of health and vigour throughout the body. This is positive thinking on a grand scale – and therein lies its value, perhaps, for most of us.

Suggestions for daily practice

This book has provided you with a whole lot of things to do and to study. Realistically speaking, it may not always be possible to practise every day and you should not feel guilty about failing to be up at the crack of dawn each morning doing your chi kung in the open air. Some days this is not going to be possible. For many people it never will be possible. What is important, however, if you are going to take the subject at all seriously, is to practise frequently and at regularly spaced intervals. A bit like going to the gym, it is of little practical value if we miss out for several weeks, only suddenly to overdo things later on trying to make up for lost time. This is actually counterproductive and can even make us unwell! Chi kung, moreover, has a certain element of psycho-motor skill attached to it and, especially during the early stages of learning, unless you practise regularly you will simple forget what you have learned.

So a good ten-minute session around once or twice a day is what you should be aiming for. You may not achieve it but we all need a target and that really has to be the minimum to aim for. And after all, ten minutes is really not that big a deal. Even if you have to squeeze it in at the end of the day, it is time far better spent than watching most of what the TV has to offer or sitting worrying about work. Beware, however, of doing chi kung too close to bedtime, as it may prevent you from sleeping. That said, many people insist that it helps them sleep soundly. So everyone is different. Meditative chi kung, however, such as the Circulation of Energy exercises we have looked at here, can be done any time – and will help settle your thoughts, no matter where you are. Always remember, wherever or however you practise, to bring the chi back down to the *tan tien* centre at the conclusion of your session.

Always refer to the notes in Chapter 02 regarding your practice environment and make sure it is peaceful, tidy and has a good supply of fresh air. The Chinese have, over the centuries, developed a highly sophisticated knowledge of what makes for a harmonious and productive environment. This venerable body of knowledge is called *feng shui* (which we looked at a little in Chapter 01) and it has much to teach us about how we should arrange our personal space, both for work and play. In the context of chi kung, it is enough to make sure the chi can circulate freely around us, that there are no obstructions or nearby obstacles that might impede our movements. Try to have open space in front of you and some form of structure behind you – i.e. rising ground if outdoors or a nearby wall if indoors. This gives a feeling of security and calm, whereas doors or windows to the rear, or open land, can generate subtle feelings of insecurity and even anxiety.

The routine

Now here is a puzzle for you to solve. Having studied this book well by now (you have studied it well, haven't you?), you will realize that there is a certain natural order in which to do the chi kung routines outlined in Chapters 03 through to 07. I am not going to tell you what it is. You are going to have to figure it out for yourself. This order bestows a good feeling to your session and gives it a structure and a meaning beyond the merely physical exercises themselves. You don't have to stick to it every time, of course. Above all, be inventive with your practice sessions. Hopefully, you will want to go on to learn other exercises and perhaps join a chi kung class that might well teach a whole set of totally different postures. But I hope, also, that you will come to enjoy the sequence suggested within these pages. I certainly do and I hope you will also.

I hope, too, that this book has provided you with some ideas on how to look after yourself and for living in accordance with the teachings and wisdom of oriental medicine. This is, I believe, one of the most important areas that any teacher should pass on. So important, in fact, that here is a brief résumé. Remember, unless you pay at least some attention to these points, your chi kung practice will be largely wasted in terms of maintaining good health:

- Eat breakfast every morning.
- Try to ensure that a high proportion of your food is cooked and warm, especially in winter.
- Take adequate rest. No disgrace in a catnap during the day.
- Strive towards honesty and integrity in all areas of life.
- Avoid extremes of climate – heat, cold, damp etc.
- Avoid extremes of emotion – anger, fear, grief etc.
- Make sure you move your bowels at least once a day.
- Know your capacity for exertion and for sexual activity.
- Moderation in all things.

Going forward

You may have realized by now that the meditation described in this chapter, the Circulation of Energy, is itself, like the *Tao*, a journey – in this case the journey of the energy around the body. It is also sometimes compared to the cycle of the seasons, the rising of chi in the *Du Mai* as the seasons of spring and summer, while the chi sinking and returning to the *tan tien* represents the autumn and winter. You may also view it as the cycle of life, from youth to old age.

> *Returning is the motion of the Tao.*
>
> *Tao Te Ching*

Your chi kung practice, therefore, is symbolic of so much that is at large in the world of nature, putting you in tune with all the great cycles and rhythms of life in a way which is quite wonderful. The chi kung experience is a journey into the infinite, a great journey to the source of things. Some days you go further than others. Some days you seem to be going into reverse. But as long as you remain on the path, your personal *tao*, you will be growing, evolving all the while.

Much of your chi kung journey will also be one in which you will, by necessity, have to make choices – not necessarily about what is good chi kung but what is good teaching. It is not always easy to determine this. Best to judge the quality of the chi kung you are being taught by how it makes you feel inside after doing it for a while, say a few weeks at least. If the teacher is generous and free with his or her knowledge and skills, and if you feel better for the experience, then it's definitely worth pursuing. It is important to respond to these inner promptings, however, and to vote with your feet if necessary. Be choosy in what you finally settle on and where you decide to 'dig the well' otherwise you will have little to show for your efforts apart from an empty wallet or purse and a lot of wasted time.

Remember, above all that chi kung is not about competing with anybody. It is not about having more of something, more chi, than anybody else, or of being more powerful and mysterious than anybody else. Neither is it really about turning your back on life and going off into isolation to find 'enlightenment'. It is in fact about sharing in something universal, something magical and yet remarkably simple which is around and within us all at every moment of our lives. And sharing, of course, is a two-way process. By developing our own chi there can be only one worthwhile outcome, and that is to help transform ourselves and our environment, no matter in how small a way, into something better, something more useful, more gentle and kind.

And now all that remains is for me to wish you well. Your journey may or may not have commenced with this small book, but I hope it has helped in shedding a little light on what to many might seem a hidden art. It isn't, of course. Chi kung is there for all of us to enjoy and marvel at. Our thanks to those who have gone before, therefore, and good wishes to all who will follow.

Bubbling Spring   Major energy centre on the soles of the feet.

chi (also written as qi)   The life force or vital energy that flows through all living things.

chi kung (also written as qi gong)   The art of circulating chi through breathing and movement.

Chinese clock   Twenty-four hour cyculation of energy through all the major organs and channels of the body. Each organ has its peak time and, 12 hours later, its low point.

Dai Mai   Major energy channel that flows around the waist.

Du Mai   Major energy channel located in the centre of the back.

elements   Abstract forces that combine many different aspects of nature and life. They are used extensively in oriental medical theory and relate to the organs of the body as well as to many other diverse subjects such as the seasons and even the tastes of food.

feng shui   Meaning simply 'wind water'. This is the ancient art of design and placement in which it is thought that chi flows through both external landscapes and within buildings and gardens. As with the human body, harmony is achieved when the chi-flow is unimpeded and yet gentle.

gu chi   Chi generated from the process of digestion.

Jing   The finite essence of the individual, essential to the production of chi in the body. Associated with the adrenal glands and sexuality.

Jingluo   The whole network of channels and vessels through which chi flows in the body.

Li and **K'an**   These are the Fire and Water centres in the body. Much of chi kung is aimed at bringing these two opposite forces into harmony.

Nei Jing   Classic text on medical theory.

oriental medicine   A term encompassing several ancient healing arts such as acupunture and herbalism that work through regulating the flow of chi throughout the body. Chi kung, therefore, shares many of the principles of oriental medical theory and can affect the health and well-being in a similar way.

Palace of Weariness   Despite the name, this is a major energy centre in the palm of the hand.

Po   Vigorous life force and physical sensation. Associated with the energy of the Lungs.

Ren Mai   Major energy channel located in the centre line of the front of the body.

shiatsu   A massage therapy, from Japan, than stimulates the flow of chi through the muscles and tendons through a combination of stretching and the application of pressure.

Shen   The vital spirit or 'mind' in oriental medical theory. Associated with the energy of the Heart.

Tai Chi T'u (or double fish diagram)   This is the famous divided circle symbol. It represents the harmony and interchange of opposites so central to the practice of exercises such as chi kung.

Taoism   The enduring philosophy of Chinese culture that emphasizes detachment and calm – ideal, therefore, for understanding the thought-process underlying exercises such as chi kung.

tan tien   Vital centre located in the lower abdomen and from which the movements of chi kung are directed.

Tao Te Ching   Classic text on Taoist philosophy.

wei chi   Defensive, protective chi, associated with the immune system.

yang   Abstract force of nature (opposite to Yin) that relates to many diverse experiences such as expansion, advance, light, activity, external strength and conscious thought.

Yi   Mental focus. The capacity for applied thinking. Associated with the energy of the Spleen.

yin Abstract force of nature (opposite to yang) that relates to many diverse experiences such as contraction, retreat, darkness, mystery, inner strength and intuition.

ying chi Refined energy that circulates around the body to nourish the organs and all the phisiological processes of the body.

Zhi Will power. The desire to undertake things. Associated with the energy of the Kidneys.

taking it further

The author's web site on chi kung can be found on

http://www.chikungwebsite.fsnet.co.uk

This site is updated regularly and, if you have enjoyed this book, you may find something of interest there, including details of video and audio tapes on chi kung and related subjects. If you do not have access to the internet, however, send a stamped addressed envelope to:

PO Box 38
Ventnor
PO38 12N
UK

For those looking to find classes in chi kung, the internet is a rich source of infomation. Just go to any search engine and type in chi kung. Beginners should also try their local adult education centre to see if it offers classes. Many now do. These are ideal for those just starting out and are usually excellent value for money.

index

teach yourself®

Afrikaans
Access 2002
Accounting, Basic
Alexander Technique
Algebra
Arabic
Árabic Script, Beginner's
Aromatherapy
Astronomy
Bach Flower Remedies
Bengali
Better Chess
Better Handwriting
Biology
Body Language
Book Keeping
Book Keeping & Accounting
Brazilian Portuguese
Bridge
Buddhism
Buddhism, 101 Key Ideas
Bulgarian
Business Studies
Business Studies, 101 Key Ideas
C++
Calculus
Calligraphy
Cantonese
Card Games
Catalan
Chemistry, 101 Key Ideas
Chess
Chi Kung
Chinese
Chinese, Beginner's

Chinese Language, Life & Culture
Chinese Script, Beginner's
Christianity
Classical Music
Copywriting
Counselling
Creative Writing
Crime Fiction
Croatian
Crystal Healing
Czech
Danish
Desktop Publishing
Digital Photography
Digital Video & PC Editing
Drawing
Dream Interpretation
Dutch
Dutch, Beginner's
Dutch Dictionary
Dutch Grammar
Eastern Philosophy
ECDL
E-Commerce
Economics, 101 Key Ideas
Electronics
English, American (EFL)
English as a Foreign Language
English, Correct
English Grammar
English Grammar (EFL)
English, Instant, for French Speakers
English, Instant, for German Speakers
English, Instant, for Italian Speakers
English, Instant, for Spanish Speakers

English for International Business
English Language, Life & Culture
English Verbs
English Vocabulary
Ethics
Excel 2002
Feng Shui
Film Making
Film Studies
Finance for non-Financial Managers
Finnish
Flexible Working
Flower Arranging
French
French, Beginner's
French Grammar
French Grammar, Quick Fix
French, Instant
French, Improve your
French Language, Life & Culture
French Starter Kit
French Verbs
French Vocabulary
Gaelic
Gaelic Dictionary
Gardening
Genetics
Geology
German
German, Beginner's
German Grammar
German Grammar, Quick Fix
German, Instant
German, Improve your
German Language, Life & Culture
German Verbs
German Vocabulary
Go
Golf
Greek
Greek, Ancient
Greek, Beginner's
Greek, Instant
Greek, New Testament
Greek Script, Beginner's
Guitar
Gulf Arabic
Hand Reflexology
Hebrew, Biblical
Herbal Medicine
Hieroglyphics
Hindi
Hindi, Beginner's
Hindi Script, Beginner's

Hinduism
History, 101 Key Ideas
How to Win at Horse Racing
How to Win at Poker
HTML Publishing on the WWW
Human Anatomy & Physiology
Hungarian
Icelandic
Indian Head Massage
Indonesian
Information Technology, 101 Key Ideas
Internet, The
Irish
Islam
Italian
Italian, Beginner's
Italian Grammar
Italian Grammar, Quick Fix
Italian, Instant
Italian, Improve your
Italian Language, Life & Culture
Italian Verbs
Italian Vocabulary
Japanese
Japanese, Beginner's
Japanese, Instant
Japanese Language, Life & Culture
Japanese Script, Beginner's
Java
Jewellery Making
Judaism
Korean
Latin
Latin American Spanish
Latin, Beginner's
Latin Dictionary
Latin Grammar
Letter Writing Skills
Linguistics
Linguistics, 101 Key Ideas
Literature, 101 Key Ideas
Mahjong
Managing Stress
Marketing
Massage
Mathematics
Mathematics, Basic
Media Studies
Meditation
Mosaics
Music Theory
Needlecraft
Negotiating
Nepali

Norwegian
Origami
Panjabi
Persian, Modern
Philosophy
Philosophy of Mind
Philosophy of Religion
Philosophy of Science
Philosophy, 101 Key Ideas
Photography
Photoshop
Physics
Piano
Planets
Planning Your Wedding
Polish
Politics
Portuguese
Portuguese, Beginner's
Portuguese Grammar
Portuguese, Instant
Portuguese Language, Life & Culture
Postmodernism
Pottery
Powerpoint 2002
Presenting for Professionals
Project Management
Psychology
Psychology, 101 Key Ideas
Psychology, Applied
Quark Xpress
Quilting
Recruitment
Reflexology
Reiki
Relaxation
Retaining Staff
Romanian
Russian
Russian, Beginner's
Russian Grammar
Russian, Instant
Russian Language, Life & Culture
Russian Script, Beginner's
Sanskrit
Screenwriting
Serbian
Setting up a Small Business
Shorthand, Pitman 2000
Sikhism
Spanish
Spanish, Beginner's
Spanish Grammar
Spanish Grammar, Quick Fix

Spanish, Instant
Spanish, Improve your
Spanish Language, Life & Culture
Spanish Starter Kit
Spanish Verbs
Spanish Vocabulary
Speaking on Special Occasions
Speed Reading
Statistical Research
Statistics
Swahili
Swahili Dictionary
Swedish
Tagalog
Tai Chi
Tantric Sex
Teaching English as a Foreign Language
Teaching English One to One
Teams and Team-Working
Thai
Time Management
Tracing your Family History
Travel Writing
Trigonometry
Turkish
Turkish, Beginner's
Typing
Ukrainian
Urdu
Urdu Script, Beginner's
Vietnamese
Volcanoes
Watercolour Painting
Weight Control through Diet and
  Exercise
Welsh
Welsh Dictionary
Welsh Language, Life & Culture
Wills and Probate
Wine Tasting
Winning at Job Interviews
Word 2002
World Faiths
Writing a Novel
Writing for Children
Writing Poetry
Xhosa
Yoga
Zen
Zulu